The Faster I Drive, The Harder It Rains

KRISTEN ROGERS

To Phill, whose happy soul is infectious,
and who is quick to remind me that
without him this book wouldn't exist.

CONTENTS

INTRODUCTION

Relationships with siblings are complex. It doesn't matter who we are or how close we are to our brothers or sisters. Maybe they are so intricate because siblings are a part of our lives for so long. Or maybe it is because of the way siblings can push each others buttons like no one else. Whatever it is, there are many layers to those relationships, and anyone with brothers or sisters experiences these complexities throughout their lives.

Sometimes relationships with siblings are close — sisters who call each other on the phone every day, tell each other everything, and trust each other implicitly. Sometimes these relationships are strained — brothers who don't talk for months or years at a time because of some real or perceived slight. Siblings can be close in age or have a decade difference between them. They can be similar in temperament and nature or as opposite as day and night.

But, when a brother or a sister has a disability — physically, developmentally or emotionally — another huge element is thrown into the mix that makes the sibling relationship even more complicated.

Few people think about the power of sibling relationships, which is ironic considering that our brothers and sisters are probably the people we will know the longest in this world. Siblings are the ones who shared all our childhood memories. They experienced the sheer joy of racing through the park to reach the swings first and the feel of hot sand between fingers in the sandbox. They felt our pain when our bike skidded out in the beauty bark, and knew the fear of having to tell Mom and Dad that someone was bleeding.

They are the ones with whom we shared our grief over the loss of the family pet, and they are the ones who hid with us in the bushes

1

when it was getting dark on one of those perfect summer evenings when we just weren't ready to go in. They were a part of every birthday party, every family funeral, all the breakups of school crushes and college romances.

They are also the people who will be with us all the way through adulthood. Siblings often outlast friends and sometimes spouses. They outlive parents, and they endure, year after year as an integral part of our lives. And yet, we often ignore these relationships, figuring that our brothers and sisters have always been around and they always will be.

Much of the time we do not consider them at all, but these are the people who help form who we are as human beings. Often they dictate, in part, the roles we take on in life and the people we become as adults. What happens to them impacts our lives whether we want it to — and whether we know it — or not.

When you have a brother or a sister with a disability, the relationship between siblings inherently gains another layer of complexity. In the case of autism in particular, there is a power differential that exists beyond any that comes naturally from birth order or age differences, and in fact, that often transcends chronological age. The siblings without autism take on a level of responsibility that is usually above and beyond that acknowledged between typical brothers and sisters.

Often, particularly when a sibling's disability is life-long, like autism, there is an understanding that responsibility for that brother or sister does not end when they become an adult. The line between sibling and parent or caregiver can become very blurred when you have a brother or sister with a disability, and that murkiness can make the job of defining the sibling's role in a family even more difficult.

This book is intended to shed some light on the often-ignored issue of the role of a typically developing sibling in the life of their brother or sister with autism, both as it exists currently and as it may manifest itself in the future.

The feelings, good and bad, that exist in relation to a brother or sister with autism are discussed. It is important to acknowledge these emotions as a person considers taking on even more responsibility for a sibling. Because each individual needs to make a conscious decision whether or not to eventually become a sibling's caretaker, I offer some pertinent questions to consider when making that choice.

Regardless of the decision that the typical sibling makes personally, a significant portion of this book is devoted to things to consider when planning the future for the sibling with autism. This is intended to help families think through all of their options and as many of the eventualities and possibilities that may arise in the lifetime of a person with autism.

The purpose of this book is to support everyone — the typical sibling, the one with autism, and the parents — to anticipate tomorrow and beyond with more confidence.

FOREWORD
BY PHILL ROGERS

I'm glad my sister wrote this book. She asked a lot of questions that help me understand myself better, and she let me see into my future, which is not something I do very often. I have learned a lot about her and about myself because she wanted to understand better.

The book is a good insight into how the other sibling (without autism) is thinking. I sense it has been a long, tough experience for Kristen to be writing this. It has been no easy task, that's for sure. It has taken a long time, and sometimes it freaked Kristen out — like how much time it has taken me to get around to writing this foreword. I'm glad this book is almost done.

For me it has been interesting seeing the things she has been putting in the book. Seeing the details of my life in writing has been kind of a shock — I didn't entirely expect some of it. It has also been hard for me to come up with some of the things she wants information about, because I'm sometimes a lazy person, and I put it off. I know the information I've given Kristen has been a big help to complete the book; in a way, without me, there would be no book, and you'd be reading a blank page.

The book has helped our relationship to grow to a better understanding of each other and how we see each other. It has increased our sensitivity to how much time we can spend together before we want to throw each other out of the car and keep on driving. It's a stronger bond now, partly because of the book, because she's gotten to know how I tick and why I do some of the things I do. I've learned some of the things I do that bug her. I try to control those things, but, as you know, with autism, sometimes it's quite hard to do what I intend.

Other people will get a better understanding about how to include the sibling with a disability in decisions that affect the future... I think this book can be useful for all families who have a person with disabilities, not just autism.

I have gained a better understanding of my impact on other people and how other people are impacted by the way I behave. I've always flown by the seat of my pants, not understanding that people want me to take a straight path, while I'm taking a path that follows a lazy S. I can see some of the ways my path bothers them. I always thought I was taking the easy path, and now I understand that my path is slightly harder because it doesn't follow what everyone else is doing.

It wasn't until recently that I've understood that things can be done differently, slower, not rushing through. Sometimes I have to push myself because it's so hard to get myself started. Even though I have a hundred different ideas, I have to push myself to jump off the cliff to get started on any of them. Even though I know I have a parachute, I have to force myself to get started, and it's not easy.

My sister has always been a person I can count on. She has helped me learn things. She has included me in her activities with her friends. She even helped me get a job where she worked.

We're very different. I'm a boy and I have autism and ADHD. I'm not like everyone else she's used to. I talk loud. I make noises. I do things my own way. Sometimes my sister bugs me when she tries to run my life or gets mad at me over dumb things. But still, she is there for me, like no one else is, even when I annoy her to pieces. It's often that people get mad at the person with disabilities for their behavior, or at the disability for causing some of the behavior. Kristen knows about that, and she watches for places to protect me from people who don't understand.

There are two sides of a disability — the side that revolves around the person who has the disability and the side around those who don't. Most families focus on the disability, learning everything about it in order to help make it have less impact. Many families do not notice what it is like for the person who does not have the disability. I recommend this book to parents that wonder about the child without a disability and what they're thinking. I recommend it to anyone who wants to see a disability from the "other" side of it.

I hope, along with Kristen, that this book will help families find their way to a plan for the future that lets everyone feel included and safe.

PHILL

I looked over at my younger brother Phill as we walked out of the house. He was wearing what he considered a typical outfit. For a few years he attended a special school in Minnesota and held a "job" where he had to sort and fold donations at the Goodwill. In Phill's mind, this created the perfect opportunity to expand his wardrobe. He had a number of interesting ensembles that came from this job, and that day's outfit was no exception.

Because the weather was chilly, he wore a collared, long-sleeved, button-down, silk shirt underneath another button-down, short-sleeved shirt with a collar that had Spiderman splashed across the front. He wore black shoes with big silver buckles that were a size too big, but that he said "really feel ok". On his head sat a black and white camouflage visor that was cinched so tight that his hair sprayed out of the top like a park fountain.

To complete the get-up, he sported various accessories. The tail of his braided-leather belt reached halfway down the side of his leg, as it had been stretched to almost twice its original length. Everything on his person that was adjustable was cinched so tight you would think he was soldering a wound.

He wore two necklaces: one, a leather rope with a buffalo tooth he found on a trip through Yellowstone Park; the other a necklace with bracelet made of puka shells that he got from our grandmother's jewelry box and screwed together to make a necklace that fit.

He wore four rings, mostly of his own creation, spread across both hands. One was his high school class ring, but the others were primarily cobbled together from 25-cent machine winnings. One had a Superman emblem glued to the top of a ring with the stone missing. A smaller plain band was wedged underneath to make it fit on his finger properly.

And, at his side, like a trusty retriever, was a messenger bag packed full of items that he never left the house without. The bag is with him always, and I have no idea what might be inside. Even if I knew, there is no way I would understand why those particular items needed to go with him.

Finally, strung around his waist were his most prized possessions that appeared to most people like some kind of high-tech utility belt: his cell phone, digital camera, iPod and hand-me-down PalmPilot with a keyboard that he won on eBay. He said he needed all this stuff to feel "normal" and that having these items with him at all times, strapped to his body, calmed him.

It doesn't matter where we were going; that was a typical outfit either for a three-day stay at my house or a trip to the movies. Each event took the same amount of preparation time and required the same accessories.

My brother is thirty-one years old, and has high-functioning autism.

An Odd Duck

Just to look at Phill you wouldn't know he has autism. You would certainly know he is a little bit different, someone my mom would refer to as an "odd duck", but you probably would not guess what was "wrong" with him. To complicate determining an accurate diagnosis, Phill also has been labeled with Attention Deficit Hyperactivity Disorder (ADHD) which is the classification he actually grew up with.

He looks in the general direction of whoever is speaking to him, though he avoids eye contact, and usually responds when spoken to. He seems to be shy or a little rude, since he doesn't automatically say hello or smile when he sees someone he knows. He participates in conversation with the people he is with, though often at an inappropriate decibel, and typically by interrupting.

Sometimes he appears to be participating in the conversation, although if you listen carefully, you realize he is only speaking to person he knows the best and often about a topic not quite the same as that being discussed by the whole group. Regularly he discusses things that are not appropriate in public —bathroom humor, an attribute of the person in front of you at the coffee shop, or some embarrassing private story (usually about you, not him) that he can repeat verbatim.

One of his favorite stories is about me. I would personally prefer he not tell it to every single person that we meet, however....

When he was three, Phill decided to run away from home. At least, that is what I assumed he had decided, since he still didn't talk. He ran at full speed down our gravel road towards the main highway (about a mile away, so he had quite a lot of running to do). I was six, and didn't think through how far he would have to go to actually "run away", or the fact that he would probably get bored or tired or both and quickly turn around. In my fear and panic-riddled state, I picked up a rock with the intention to throw it off to Phill's right side to scare him into turning around.

In order to understand this story fully, there is one important thing you need to know about me: I have absolutely no aim whatsoever. So, it was completely without malice or intention that I managed to pick up that rock, throw it, and hit my brother squarely in the back of the head. Suddenly, his white-blond hair was scarlet red, and he was screaming. He did, however, stop running.

Our neighbor, a very patient young man a few years older than me, came running over, picked up Phill, and carried him into our house. My mother took one look at my hysterically screaming brother, the blood, and my stricken face, and flew into action, putting Phill in the bathtub while she tried to control the blood and stop the bleeding, simultaneously trying to find out from me what happened.

I did what I think any six-year-old who was only trying to help a nonverbal brother would do — I lied. I told my mom that Phill had tripped and fallen over backwards and hit his head on a very pointy rock. To my great dismay, she bought it. When I was fourteen, I finally told my family the truth about what had really happened. It was then that I found out Phill ultimately had to have stitches because of that fateful rock. Apparently I had blocked that out of my mind completely.

I share this story for a couple of reasons. For one, it is an event about which I felt incredibly embarrassed and guilty for years. For another, it became something my brother instinctively has felt the need to bring up in every social situation ever since.

Honestly, he tells this story to everyone we meet — usually just as he is introduced to them, with no clarification of what he is talking about. Sometimes he simply offers some reference to how I tried to kill him or threw rocks at his head. If anyone looks at him inquisitively, or innocently asks what he means by his comments, he is more than happy to dive into the full blown story, with me as the mean-hearted sister out for blood — literally. It is embarrassing to me, and it is a constant signature of Phill's manifestation of autism. He is obsessed with telling stories about other people, regardless of whether they want him to or not (and usually they don't).

Another reason I want to share this particular anecdote is to demonstrate Phill's unexpected sense of humor. Once I resigned myself to hearing this story whenever new people entered our lives, I started filling in the blanks of the story and adding my own spin on it so that I didn't appear quite so evil. During one particular telling, Phill and I were sitting at an outdoor table at Starbucks with my boss and a co-worker. Phill started telling the story, and I added my two cents, and everyone laughed about the story. Phill was quiet for a second and then looked at me and grinned. He turned back to our audience and said, "Hey! Maybe hitting me in the head with a rock is what made me autistic! Yeah, I was just fine before — it wasn't until after you hit me with the rock that I got the diagnosis!" After a minute of stunned silence, everyone at the table started laughing uncontrollably. His timing was perfect, and he looked so earnest — it was truly a great joke. However, now whenever he tells that story he ends it with, "...and that's why I'm autistic", and people who didn't hear the original delivery just look stunned and concerned. Phill really does have a great sense of humor; he just doesn't always know when and where to use it.

Sometimes the evidence of Phill's autism is obvious. The lack of eye contact, the strange noises, the inappropriate comments, his gait, and his outfit choices, all of these things suggest that something is just a little different with Phill. Other times, however, his disabilities are far more subtle.

Recently I had two experiences that reminded me that Phill has difficulties navigating this world that I don't even fathom most of the time. The first was one day as we drove to my office where Phill worked two days a week. Phill was telling me about a story he had heard on the radio or CNN. He was telling it to me word for word at seven o'clock in the morning, and I was struggling to keep track of the details. As he relayed the fascinating nugget of wisdom he had gleaned from this news blurb, he got to a portion of the story where the news anchor had referenced something about a nickel. Phill stopped, looked at me, and said, "Wait — is a nickel ten cents?" I faltered for a second and then assured him that a nickel was five cents. To which he answered, "Oh, right. A dime is ten cents, right?"

A few days later we were driving home from work during a torrential downpour when Phill made an observation about the weather. He said, "Have you ever noticed that it rains harder the faster you drive?" Again I was struck by this comment and a bit taken back. We had a long conversation about why it might seem like it rains harder as you drive faster, even though it doesn't actually, but Phill wasn't completely convinced by my arguments.

Neither of these stories is intended to make Phill seem unintelligent, because that is far from the truth. He is very smart and inquisitive. However, there are concepts that simply elude him, concepts that would seem obvious to others and that can impact how he is able to navigate life in ways that others might forget to consider. Not knowing how much each coin in his hand represents can have major day-to-day implications, and is not something that strangers think to help with. On the other hand, it is also something that Phill can compensate for, and often has, by simply paying with a bill and not worrying about change.

These are the types of issues I never even consider in my daily life, and these interactions with Phill remind me how much more confusing the world must seem to him than it does to me. The greater lesson to be learned from these situations is that Phill orders his life in a way that is far different than the way most of us make sense of the world.

Phill wasn't formally diagnosed with autism until he was 21. Certainly we were aware there was something different about him, and he previously had been given diagnoses that ranged from ADHD and learning disabled, to bipolar and schizophrenic. For most of his life our family used the ADHD label to get him through school and to explain his behavior to others. When he was seven or eight, my mom coined the term "ADHD Plus" to describe Phill, since he behaved more strangely than the other children with ADHD.

For my parents, the awareness of Phill's challenges came at different times. When Phill was seven-and-a-half months old, my mom asked Phill's doctor for a referral to a specialist. Despite the doctor's assurances, she knew that he was not matching the descriptions in child raising books and was not behaving like I did as an infant. Mostly, however, she was concerned about his size (he was very small) and his eating (he was spitting up just about everything he ate). At that time, he was diagnosed with an immature pyloric valve which was the reason given for both his small stature and the spitting up.

A little later my parents took Phill to another doctor because my mom was concerned he wasn't meeting developmental milestones. He was diagnosed with developmental delays in language, motor, and cognitive skills, and the doctors also noted a strong chance that he had ADHD.

Based on the analysis by those doctors, Phill went into speech and occupational therapy and started early intervention preschool, which serves developmentally delayed children. By then, my mom observed that Phill's "parallel play" was very evident. He would play in the room with other children, but he never really played with them. Even more interesting was his need to line up all of his toys all of the time. He didn't play with his toys so much as arrange them. Now we know that these are clear signs of autism, but they were downplayed at the time.

When Phill was five, my mom wanted to put him on medication for ADHD, and my dad was unsure about this choice. They took him to another developmental diagnostic center in Seattle. There it was evident that he had ADHD and needed more services. Ironically, it seems that the ADHD was part of the reason Phill's autism was diagnosed so late. At that time, autism symptoms were primarily understood as a child who was withdrawn, physically and emotionally, nonverbal, and did not engage with the environment. Phill was the absolute antithesis of this description. He was a very happy baby — smiling, gurgling, and interacting with people around him. He was also incredibly active. Every person who encountered him and every doctor and practitioner who saw him commented on it. In all of my mom's notes about his development, she talks about how he was getting into things and playing with things and moving, moving, moving. This simply was not the picture of autism as it was known in the early 1990s.

My dad says that he worked very hard not to see a problem for a number of years. Looking back, he can see definite signs that something was different about Phill. When one of my parents would pick up baby Phill, he didn't nuzzle into their necks, but instead put a tiny hand in the middle of their chests and pushed off, twisting around to see what else was around him, instead of engaging with his caretaker.

He didn't crawl like most children either. When he became mobile, Phill rolled everywhere he wanted to go, and then eventually moved to pulling his body across the floor with his arms and elbows like a soldier in a foxhole. Despite these clues, our dad says that he spent more time looking for normal behaviors than noticing abnormal behaviors, and that he was "cursed with an optimism" that was reinforced by a lot of people in his life.

It wasn't until Phill was five and they took him to the specialists in Seattle that my dad was able to acknowledge that his son's development was definitely atypical. Even then he held onto the idea that Phill was delayed by about two years, as opposed to being permanently impacted. I can't blame him for not wanting to believe it; who wants to believe the worst imaginable scenario for their child? Luckily my mom's persistence helped ensure that Phill received services while my dad worked through acceptance of the situation as it truly was.

When Phill was 17, I was studying abroad in London for my junior year in college when I stumbled across the diagnosis of Asperger's syndrome. A psychology major, I had certainly heard of autism, but this disorder, apparently related to autism, didn't sound like the disorder I had known at all; it wasn't just about a non-verbal child who rocks back and forth and is typically institutionalized. Nor was it the "Rainman" version of a marginally functioning savant who makes no eye contact, repeats words and phrases, and can, in a matter of seconds, calculate the number of toothpicks left in a box after the box is spilled. This new definition was more flexible and covered different levels of autism, along with a type of autism that existed in people who interacted with the world on a daily basis. More importantly, Asperger's syndrome described a set of symptoms and behaviors that, for the first time, accurately described my brother.

I called home the night I read about Asperger's to tell my mom about my amazing discovery. Somewhere in the back of my mind, I thought I had single-handedly discovered the key that would set my brother free from the difficult life he had experienced thus far. In my daydream, with this new diagnosis he, and we, would suddenly understand what was going on with him, and we would realize that a world of resources and services existed for kids like Phill: a new school where he would flourish, a place where he would make friends with people like himself, and an understanding that would make us accept Phill and all of his quirky behaviors unconditionally. I think somewhere deep down I even thought that with this diagnosis I would stop being annoyed by the volume at which he talked and the way he interrupted constantly to talk about himself, by the noises he made for no apparent reason, and the outfits he wore out in public.

When I told my mom what I had discovered, she said "Oh yeah, I've known about Asperger's for a while. I have thought that Phill might have that for the last three or four years."

I was stunned and totally deflated. I thought maybe she had misunderstood. I read her the symptoms and related how they fit Phill. She agreed with me, but never mirrored my enthusiasm. I became exasperated and asked testily, "If you knew about this, why haven't you had Phill evaluated?"

We have a very loving, committed mother, and I could not believe how she had dropped the ball on this one. Her next words never left me, because no matter what my argument, her sentiment didn't change. She said "I haven't seen what having another label would do to help him."

I argued for all the new services that I envisioned and for Phill's personal awareness about himself. I thought about myself and what I would want to know about how my own mind worked. But my mom didn't see any compelling reason to take him to the doctor. That was in part because those types of resources didn't exist then for someone as high-functioning as Phill. Because he had a normal IQ and was verbal, he wouldn't have qualified for all those fabulous programs that I imagined.

Now, looking back, I don't blame her. As a child, he was tested and tested and retested. Mom and Phill endured literally thousands of hours of tests and doctor's appointments, medication alterations, and school meetings. At seventeen, when I had my revelation, he was doing ok. He didn't have any friends, and he was by no means a stellar student, but he was on track to graduate from high school. He was mostly getting his IEP needs met. An IEP (Individual Education Program) offers each student who qualifies special education services from their school. This in itself is no small feat. Furthermore, if the school wasn't supplying the necessary services, Mom was helping him herself.

She told me later that she believed she had to get Phill through high school with his self-esteem intact, and then he would find a passion and a way in the world that worked for him. She had a brother with ADD and saw this strategy play out in his life. She had no reason to believe it wouldn't work with Phill.

In that same vein, my mom was very committed to helping Phill become as successful as he possibly could be. She constantly worried that giving him another diagnosis would be an excuse, in his mind, not to push himself past his comfort zone, and that others would write him off and not hold him to as high of standards.

I also think, at that point she was pouring all her energy into getting Phill through school, and it simply didn't occur to her that caring for Phill could last his entire lifetime. She had a husband and a career to devote time and energy to, and the idea that Phill would always need her time and efforts, as he did then, was unimaginable.

So, Phill was not diagnosed until he was a young adult and had been expelled from a life skills school. There did not seem to be a place where he fit, and he was about to lose health insurance. The school professionals were suggesting that Phill needed to live in a 24-hour supervised program for the safety of himself and others, implying that he had a mental illness such as bipolar disorder or schizophrenia.

Only then did Phill's doctors give him the official diagnosis of autism. The diagnosis was important for him to qualify for government assistance, primarily health insurance, which he needed, since he was not eligible to be on our parents' plans any longer and did not have a job that covered him.

However, even without the "official" label, in the intervening years since his high school graduation, we had begun explaining to those who asked that we believed Phill was autistic.

The new diagnosis has been a relief to some of us, most notably my father and me. It was the first and only explanation that fit Phill. We appreciate being able to put a name to Phill's behavior that both fits him (unlike the ADHD label) and that people can understand, even if only superficially.

The label was much more difficult for my mother to come to terms with, but I think she now sees it fits better. If nothing else, it removed the bipolar label which she profoundly disagreed with.

However, for Phill the new diagnosis was especially difficult. He was very confused as to why the diagnosis changed, especially since he fits the ADHD diagnosis as well as the autistic.

He told me once he doesn't have dyslexia (one of the learning disabilities he was diagnosed with as a child); he has autism. I don't think he believed me when I told him he had both. He thought it must be one or the other.

My mom's original fear that he would use the label as a crutch has also been a challenge for Phill. It is very easy for him (and for anyone with a label) to say, "I'm not good at that because I'm autistic" or "I do that because I'm autistic" and not take responsibility for his own actions. He is starting to recognize his penchant for using the diagnosis as a cop out, but it is a very difficult behavior to change. It has been challenging trying to teach him the subtleties between his autism making things more difficult for him and it making it impossible.

Phill's autism is exhausting to deal with and complicated, and yet he is relatively high functioning. The traditional diagnosis of autism is "a child totally withdrawn from the world — a child who cannot interact with anyone". I am grateful that Phill functions as well as he does and that his diagnosis is what it is. Still, I wonder if it isn't harder on him to be aware of his differences and the way people talk about him and treat him. He has lived his life beautifully — far better than I believe I could have with the challenges he was presented. I have always been impressed with his ability to grow and to push through obstacles that seem so daunting. I gain strength by watching him master his differences and come out the other side with his humor and faith intact. He certainly has days where he questions the use of his efforts, and he bemoans some of the things he can't seem to ever get a handle on, like why he can't get a girlfriend or find a job. In general, however, he believes he will prevail.

Defining Autism

Autism is difficult to accurately diagnose. A doctor can't administer a blood test, perform an MRI, or look in a patient's ears to ascertain the problem. Instead, autism is a neurological disorder made up of a constellation of symptoms of varying intensity. It presents differently depending on which symptoms a person has and how severe each characteristic is.

The National Institute of Mental Health (NIMH) states that: "all children with ASD (Autistic Spectrum Disorders) demonstrate deficits in 1) social interaction, 2) verbal and nonverbal communication, and 3) repetitive behaviors and interests. In addition, they will often have unusual responses to sensory experiences, such as certain sounds or the way objects look." They also state these symptoms "will present in each individual child differently".

Autism typically begins prior to three years of age, but usually isn't diagnosed until about then, though advances in the science of understanding autism have increased the percentage of children who are diagnosed earlier — sometimes at as young an age as eighteen months. The difference between Asperger's syndrome and autism is primarily the evidence of a delay during language development. Individuals with high functioning autism can look very similar to individuals with Asperger's. The difference will be that people with Asperger's learn to speak at an age-appropriate time without difficulty.

The technical descriptions of the manifestations of the disorder are as follows: repeating words and phrases in place of normal, responsive language; difficulty understanding and responding to the emotional needs of others; obsessive attachment to objects; difficulty in creating and maintaining friendships; or repetitive and/or odd play. In my mind, a list in a book or on a website of the criteria for autism does not draw a clear picture of a person who carries the autism label. Phill is not a set of symptoms; he is a person. But he does have autism.

Here is what it looks like in real life: "difficulty in creating or maintaining friendships". In Phill's life, that means he has never had any real friends, except for the few years he spent at Minnesota Life College with other developmentally delayed and ADHD kids. During his entire childhood, growing up, he never had a sleepover. He never brought a friend home from school. He went to a few birthday parties in kindergarten and first grade when kids invited the whole class, but since then none. Now he participates in activities with his mom, with me, and with my friends, when I invite him along.

Phill demonstrates "difficulty understanding and responding to the emotional needs of others" when he doesn't give me a hug if I am crying, or tell me he hopes I feel better, or that he understands why I am upset. He either changes the subject entirely (I'm sitting on the couch crying and Phill will look at me and say "Did you see American Chopper last night? They were building this really cool bike...") or he will tell me how much harder things are for him than they are for me. ("I know you are sad because you didn't get the job you want, but think about me; I mean, I don't even have a job. That is a lot worse.")

Recently he and I have worked on the social reciprocity piece, but it is definitely a wholly learned and not even remotely innate set of skills for him. Phill doesn't hold doors open for women — or men, for that matter. When we go out to a bar on Friday afternoons and a coworker offers to pick up the first round, Phill never offers to pick up the next round, or any round. We have been talking about how that is what you do if you want to be invited out again, but it is not something that comes naturally to him.

I can't even begin to describe the extent to which "repeating words and phrases in place of normal, responsive language" occurs in our daily lives. Sometimes Phill sits in the back of the car and says a phrase over and over — usually a made-up or especially silly fragment: "giggle tickle fart... giggle tickle fart..." or he will use a word for a day, or a week or a month, for almost everything. During the time that I was looking for a new house, he coined the term "crack shackle" for a very run-down, beat-up home and then used it consistently about any home and most people for about a month and a half.

He expresses obsessive behavior as well. As a child, when he was about five, he became totally obsessed with Superman and called everyone Clark Kent. Our babysitter, our mom, the guy at the gas station, everyone.

The obsession with Superman brings us to another of Phill's manifestations of autism: "repetitive behaviors and interests". Superman was one of those repetitive interests for Phill. When we saw one of the Christopher Reeve versions of the movie, he was hooked. He wore Superman pajamas; he played "Superman" and watched Superman cartoons. He had Superman books, bedsheets, and underwear. That Christmas he asked only for Superman and other superhero action figures; he received at least six of each character (eight Batman, thirteen Superman, six Wonder Woman, etc.) but he wouldn't return any. Every time he opened another package with yet another superhero in it, he shouted "thank you!" with true enthusiasm as he added it to the pile.

His obsession wasn't like other kids who like a particular character or movie. It wasn't something he paid attention to only when he played or when he went to bed. Remember those pajamas I mentioned? They had a cape that attached with Velcro. Every day for two to three years, Phill wore that Superman pajama shirt to day care, cape and all. My mom could barely pull it off him to wash.

Phill had growth hormone deficiency as a kid, meaning that he was always very small and didn't grow in normal spurts like other kids, so that shirt fit him for a long, long time. In fact, though the fascination is less intense, he is still focused on Superman. He has a ring and a necklace bearing the Superman emblem, and he often carts around a hardback book about the franchise of Superman. I don't know that he has ever read the whole thing, but he loves just having that tome by his side.

And it isn't just Superman. Phill moves from one intensive fascination to another; Mom describes it as where his ADHD hits his autism. Unlike many children with autism who have one preoccupation for their entire lives, Phill has significant periods of time where he is intensely focused on one thing like Superman, and then he stops and moves to his next fascination, many of which are related to movies of some kind.

During his "Back to the Future" phase, he crafted an outfit that looked like the one Michael J. Fox wore as Marty McFly — jeans, a plaid, button-down shirt, and suspenders. He wore it to school every day. He wanted to sleep in it, like Marty did, but Mom made him remove it so she could launder it.

The "Teen Wolf" period was particularly difficult for me to explain to people, though it was Mom's favorite because she thought he looked so cute. For Halloween one year he went as Teen Wolf, with a wolf mask, gloves with fur on them, and a corduroy jacket with patches on the sleeves. He wanted to wear that all the time too. Because the mask posed a bit of a challenge, he often wore only the hairy hands.

Now, whenever he gets dressed, Phill has to tighten every adjustable piece of his clothing to the point that it practically cuts off circulation. I am not sure if this is part of the repetitive behavior or a different manifestation of his autism, but it is a self-imposed requirement. When he removes his hat, there are deep red lines on his head, and he breaks a pair of shoelaces about every six months. I asked him why he makes everything so tight, and he said it is because it makes him feel weighted down. For him, it is a sense of being present in the world, and it makes him feel secure. I think Phill may feel every day like you or I do when we take prescription pain medications. It is a kind of disconnected, light-headed, loopy feeling. I believe that Phill tightens everything down so that he can pull himself out of that feeling and into reality.

The NIMH notes that "subtle social cues" — whether a smile, a wink, or a grimace — may have little meaning to a person with autism. To a child who misses these cues, "Come here" always means the same thing, whether the speaker is smiling and extending arms for a hug or frowning and planting fists on the hips. Without the ability to interpret gestures and facial cues, the social world may feel bewildering.

If, when we look at someone, we have no clue as to whether they are happy or mad about what we had just done, it would create a world of confusion and fear for most of us, and that is how people with autism live every day. They do not get cues from our tone of voice or the smiles or scowls on our faces to help them make sense of a situation.

In college, I had a professor tell me that stereotypes are important and are the way we organize the world. One example she gave was driving. When we are driving down the road, we have a belief — a stereotype — that the cars coming towards us are going to drive only in their own lane; they are not going to careen into our lane. Part of this belief is the assumption that others believe what we believe, that everyone should be driving in their own lane. If we did not believe this and, instead, had to question and assess the intentions of every driver coming towards us, we would never get anywhere. We'd pull over every time a car was driving near us.

Phill has certain beliefs about the world that are not the same as those of the people around him, like that it rains harder the faster you drive. Consequently, he is constantly surprised by the way things happen. He seems even more perplexed if he is in a group of people and all of the people around him appear to mysteriously believe that things will happen the same way. Confusing to him are facts such as: everyone at the table at lunch knows how much to tip the server, when it is appropriate to drink alcohol and when it isn't, and what month comes after September, although he usually doesn't spend a lot of time contemplating them. However, it does mean that most of life is unexpected — even more so than for the rest of us — and he is genuinely taken aback when people become annoyed or angry with him for something "he should have known".

He experienced frustration from others in situations like this a lot when we were kids. Our parents are divorced and both remarried. Our dad married our step-mom, Marcia, when Phill was four and our mom married our step-dad Brian when Phill was ten. This sometimes made Phill's inability to ascertain why people were upset with his behavior and what was appropriate even harder, because the rules were a little bit different depending on which house we were living in. Our step-mom Marcia is concerned with socially appropriate behavior and manners. She conducts herself with considerable etiquette and expects the same in return from the people around her. Phill never really understood mealtime manners, appropriate conversation for dinner or, most importantly, how to conduct a conversation in a way that allows other people to participate. Before we knew that this behavior was related to his diagnosis, many people, particularly Marcia, perceived it as willful disregard of the rules, the skills he had been taught, and bad manners. Marcia started removing herself from activities that required her to spend a lot of time around Phill (like dinners), and eventually gave up on the idea of having more than a surface relationship with him. He wasn't learning to be appropriate, and it was too hard for her.

Knowing that he wasn't doing things right made Phill nervous about giving the wrong answer, and instead he started using stalling techniques to buy himself some time to determine acceptable responses to questions he was asked. But not understanding when it made sense to stall, he developed the habit of doing it anytime he didn't like something or didn't want to answer a question, which led everyone to know he disapproved of whatever was going on.

He couldn't figure out how people knew he wasn't happy. In a higher than normal pitch, he would say "Hmm. I will have to think about that and get back to you." Now, unfortunately for him, that response annoys the heck out of me, and others, because what we hear is: "I don't want to tell you" or "I don't want to" or, simply, "no". Again, he has no idea why his learned response intended to appease his audience still results in annoyance.

These examples offer my ideas of how one person with autism looks, and are not meant as a set of criteria. I particularly want to clarify that Phill is not just a person with autism. He is a fascinating, quirky, fun individual.

First and Foremost, a Brother

It is easy, from many of the stories that I tell to think of Phill as a character, or a caricature. In reality, he is a regular guy with some irregular behaviors and difficulties. I want to be clear that Phill is so much more than a person with autism, and that he functions well in many situations.

While we aren't sure how he will do living autonomously, he is entirely capable of taking care of his own day-to-day needs, including meals, hygiene (when he feels like it), and basic home maintenance. He can manage his own medications, get himself to appointments, and find ways to entertain himself.

The issue with these tasks is not whether he can do them, but whether he will. When he's home for a few days in a row, he tends not to shower, and when he doesn't shower, he forgets to take his pills.

Phill can hold a job, as well. It isn't clear at this point if a full time job is a possibility, but he is certainly a hard worker, and with good supervision and direction, more than capable of being an excellent employee.

In his free time, my brother loves the same activities that other thirty-something guys enjoy. He hangs out at the mall, plays video games, goes skiing, and rides his bike. He is also an incredibly funny guy, and always has a pun or piece of observational humor ready. He usually delivers a joke with an air of complete seriousness; the only clue is the hint of a smile on his lips. If a situation is especially serious or the individual he's with seems upset, he's quick to try to lighten the mood.

In person, particularly with new people, Phill can come off as closed-off or unapproachable, but underneath that armor, he has a very happy soul and a generally easy-going way of being. When he chooses, he's happy to be with folks. He's not picky about what restaurant or movie to frequent, or what errands need to be run. His memory for detail makes him an excellent partner on outings, and he's quick with a reminder about something that's been forgotten.

He is an innately giving person. As a child, he was happy to share his toys with kids in the neighborhood; now he loves to offer a bite of an exceptionally good dish or show off his newest gadget and let others play with it. He's the first person to drop what he is doing to help if asked. Whenever I have yard work and needs a second pair of hands, Phill is happy to come over and do whatever is requested.

Kids are fascinated with Phill. When my friend, Sarah, needed a babysitter for her eighteen-month-old daughter, Isa, I was happy to oblige. However, I had Phill with me that day, so the two of us took on the responsibility of babysitting my god-daughter together. At first, as with most people and new experiences, Phill was nervous and a little skittish around Isa. He quickly settled down, and soon surprised me with his incredible skill connecting with our active little charge, showing his ability to entertain her. He got down on her level to play, choosing toys that were fun and challenging and giving her room to try to operate them by herself. He talked to her in a soothing tone, using the sing-song voice that most parents use with their children. It was fascinating to watch, and is a prime example of how he effortlessly interacts with children.

He truly adores animals of all kinds, so much so that he volunteers at the local zoo simply to observe their behavior. His ability with animals has always been evident with family pets. I have a four-pound Yorkie who adores Phill, and Phill is completely devoted to him. He takes him for walks, makes sure he has food and water, and loves to hold and brush him. When I am out of town, Phill is the first to volunteer to dog sit for me and always takes very good care of him, to the point that he cries for Phill when I get home.

That ability to connect with and care for children and animals is a fascinating way to judge the goodness in a person's character, and Phill's compassion for both are easy to ascertain. And, while he is loathe to give hugs or express any deep emotions face-to-face with people, he writes the most touching letters and emails to let others know how he feels about them.

His tenacity and fixation on a task or object can be especially useful. He rarely complains about projects he is given at work, even if they might be construed by others to be monotonous or boring. He diligently follows instructions and does his best to see a job through to the end. He gets an intense satisfaction from seeing things in his purview from start to finish, but recognizes that it takes as long as it takes.

Phill has always been active, which is related to the ADHD. Still, it is just a part of who he is. He is a skiing machine. He will go with anyone who wants to ski, and he's the first one on the hill and the last one off. His only frustration when he's on the mountain is people who don't follow the rules, people who push or cut in the chair lift lines or who ignore the rules of etiquette when skiing down a run. He chatters happily on the chair lift to the people he knows, and can be heard singing to himself while racing down the slopes. He is active to the point of utter exhaustion. He holds nothing back when skiing, hiking, or golfing.

His commitment to the present is inspiring. He lives almost entirely in the moment, not worrying about tomorrow or yesterday; he focuses all of his energy on the right now. We could probably all learn something from that ability. It affords him an extraordinary level of emotion for whatever he is engaged in, and I think helps him remember each minute with more clarity than most of us.

In fact, Phill has an incredible memory for experiences and events.

We drove across the country in a tiny motor home when Phill was nine, and he can remember details about that trip that are amazing. He knows the names of the cities and even the camping areas we stayed in, while I can barely remember that we visited the state he is mentioning.

He's a prolific photographer, but he doesn't need a camera. He can describe locations and activities as if we were there just last week. He remembers the feel and the smell, down to the road that we drove on to get to a particular place. He and our mom and Brian drove across the country again when Phill was 13. When they traveled through states he hadn't been in for four years, Phill could point down a dusty road and say, "if you drive down there a few miles, you'd be at the campsite we stayed at during that huge thunderstorm..." and he would be completely correct.

I think, however, that Phill's greatest strength is his incredibly big heart. He may not show affection in typical ways, and he may not let people into his world easily, but there can be no doubt when he trusts and loves a person. He is fiercely protective of the people in his life. He remembers the smallest details about each person's likes and dislikes, wants and desires, wishes and dreams. He practically catalogs favorite TV shows, restaurants, hobbies, and activities. He does his best to make the people around him happy, whether he knows how or not. And once you are in his circle, you are in. The love is unconditional, which is pretty unusual and an amazing gift for those of us lucky enough to experience it.

Adulthood

I do worry about the future for him, however. His anger has always been demonstrated through frustrated outbursts, but it is now magnified by his adult size and weight. During times of stress, the outbursts are more frequent, and when they occur in public, bystanders look concerned and wonder if he might become violent. Maybe the increase in frequency is because he faces greater struggles now that he is an adult, or because he has a better awareness of his own feelings and his limitations, as we all do as we grow older.

My fear is that it is because he is losing that unshakable faith he had as a child, that he is beginning to doubt he will achieve his dreams. I desperately hope that is not what is driving the change in his attitude, because I think it is what has made him such an extraordinary person.

This change in his behavior is a concern for me practically as well. I'm afraid his anger will become more and more prevalent, and I don't know how to accommodate him if that is the case. Phill says he isn't sure what is causing him to be more explosive and feel more anger, and he resists the idea of exploring the issue further. For the most part, he brushes off the outbursts and says they aren't a big deal. That may be true from his perspective, but it isn't necessarily the case for those of us on the outside.

A couple of years ago we took a vacation, my brother, my ex-husband Karl, and I flying together. At the airport upon our return, Phill was desperate for his luggage to come off the carousel first. I'm not sure why that was important, but once he had it in his head, that was how it had to be. His suitcase arrived before ours, bringing him significant satisfaction, and he headed to the oversized baggage area to await the arrival of his skis. Karl and I soon followed him with our luggage in tow. Just as we arrived, Karl's snowboard came down the ramp. Karl laughed as he picked up his stuff, seeing the frustration on Phill's face over this contest my brother had made up himself and then lost.

In hindsight, I believe Phill's anger wasn't just about the luggage. He had spent the whole weekend being told what to do by his family — Karl, my dad, our step-sister, and me. I think it took its toll. In his exasperation and frustration, he lashed out and kicked Karl in the leg. Karl responded in an angry voice and told Phill he'd better not kick him ever again. Phill is not often violent and, though he is very impulsive, he usually apologizes for inappropriate behavior almost as soon as he executes it. This time, though, he took a step towards Karl and pushed him. To Karl's credit, he did not engage Phill in this confrontation and, instead, turned and walked away. Phill, who doesn't like people to be angry with him, usually tries to placate those he has offended soon after he has blown off steam. In this case, however, he didn't apologize to Karl for a week.

I tell that story because, if it is simply an incident of an impulsive young man getting fed up with a weekend of frustrations and venting, it isn't a huge deal. He and Karl made up, and he appeared to understand that his behavior was inappropriate. But, there is a chance, in my mind, that this indicates the potential for escalation.

What if he becomes increasingly angry and this violence becomes part of his lashing out? Kicking Karl is unacceptable, but it is an action with relatively minor consequences. What if he starts kicking strangers or police officers? What if he is violent towards me, when I am his primary caretaker? He has about fifty pounds on me and is considerably stronger than I am. I don't know that I can control the situation if he is out of control and physically attacking me. I don't think Phill would explode unless he was provoked, but as this story demonstrates, it's hard to tell what my brother would consider provocation.

Since that incident, Phill's anger has subsided. In part that is due to a change in his medication, and in part he has become more aware of himself and has taken more control of his life. Phill feels that his independence has helped him have more of a say over his decisions which has, in turn, given him more power over his own emotions.

However, I cannot determine whether he will continue to have control over his anger during the next time of stress, or transition, or when Phill's independence is limited.

This is one of the many situations that I now contemplate as I carefully consider the role that I will one day take on, and as I watch my brother mature. Someday I will be my brother's keeper; I will be solely responsible for his care and wellbeing when our parents are gone. That role will be defined in part by Phill — who he is, how he behaves and the person he is becoming. It will also be greatly shaped by the person that I am and the life that I want for both myself and for Phill.

MY LIFE AS THE 'TYPICAL' SIBLING

I used to be an only child. It was just me, my mom and my dad for almost four blissful years. Then my parents had Phill. Everything changed at that time, and not only because there were two children where once there was one.

At first we had a very normal family dynamic. My parents worked hard to care for their two children, my father working outside the house and my mother working inside. My brother worked hard being a baby, and I worked hard pitching a fit that my family had been invaded and I no longer received undivided attention.

At one point a few weeks after Phill came home from the hospital, I decided that if I wasn't going to get the proper amount of attention, I should leave. I started packing up my belongings so I could run away. Fortunately I didn't quite understand running away when I was four. My mom discovered my plans when I came downstairs to ask for more boxes in order to finish packing. Eventually, like all children, I adjusted to my new role as big sister instead of only child, and relished the role. But our normality didn't last very long.

In my family, I'm the "typical" sibling. I do not have autism or Asperger's or ADHD or learning disabilities. I am what society would call "normal", but I do not want to use that word to describe myself because of the implication then that Phill is "abnormal". Therefore, I've decided to refer to myself as "typical" which refers to a typically developing person versus someone with autism whose development is atypical.

Being the "Good" Kid

My brother and I are two very different people. I am and always have been a rule follower. I just am. I was born that way. I don't lie well, I am neither comfortable with, nor adept at, doing things wrong; I would almost always prefer to be known as a "good girl". My brother is not what I would characterize as a rule breaker in that he doesn't try to do things he knows are wrong, but he has always been a very curious person and tends not to think about whether something is right or wrong but rather whether it would be fun to do. In other words, while not a rule-breaker at heart, Phill breaks the rules a fair amount of the time whether he means to or not.

There are a lot of positives to being the typical one. As a child, it was pretty easy to be the good kid most of the time. I received the best grades in school, and I was better at sports. I could talk Phill into just about anything because I seemed to know so much more about how the world worked. I was treated like an adult much of the time. This proved to be both a positive and a negative, but most of the time it was something I appreciated. I received a lot of praise for "being such a good sister" and "taking care of Phill". And, in comparison to Phill's struggles, my accomplishments seemed even more impressive.

But there are negatives to being the typical one. I received far less time with our parents as I grew up. It was understandable. Phill needed more help with his homework, needed to be driven wherever he was going because he never learned to drive, and needed to be entertained much of the time because he seldom had any friends of his own. I had friends and activities, things that filled my days and gave me companionship. Because Phill didn't have anyone to play with most of the time, our parents, and our mom in particular, spent a lot of time being Phill's friend – going to the movies, the park, the zoo, and just hanging out.

For a few years, Phill went to a special school about two hours away from our house. My mom drove him there and picked him up every single day, which took two hours each trip, so they had a lot of time, just the two of them, that I missed out on.

I was by no means abandoned. By that time my mom had remarried and we had a step-father who was good about picking me up from activities, dropping me off at school, making sure I had dinner, and all of those things. But it was not the same as the undivided attention that Phill got from our mom. And while it was completely healthy to be jealous of the extra time that Phill spent with our parents, it felt wrong to be envious of someone who had so many other challenges in his life. The hurt that came with receiving less attention became compounded by the guilt about feeling jealous.

A major negative to being the typical one was having a typical desire to fit in. I was always the one who was embarrassed by Phill's behaviors related to his autism, far more than Phill was ever bothered by them. This feels like a horrible thing to say – being embarrassed by my brother's disability – but I was, especially as a child. When we went to the grocery store and Phill started talking at the top of his lungs about the overweight woman two carts ahead of us, or would have tantrums of frustration, I wanted to sink into the floor and disappear. Sometimes I even pretended I wasn't with him, smiling sympathetically at the other store patrons about this odd boy.

When we played outside in the neighborhood, I often sent Phill home. When Mom asked him why he was back, he replied "Kristen says I am upset because the other kids are picking on me." Phill was never upset by the other kids and usually didn't even know he was being teased. But I was upset they were making fun of him; sending him home was the only way I could make them stop.

Another challenge I encountered was deciding whether or not to bring friends home from school. Once I brought a new friend home, and Phill ran through the living room wearing his wolf mask, singing a song that he created at a volume that made me want to put my hands over my ears. He was eleven. I was mortified, and figured I should never bring anyone else home again unless I was certain of their friendship and their hardiness to withstand anything.

Eventually I learned that it didn't matter what the people at the grocery store or in the neighborhood thought about Phill. I did find that bringing friends home was a good way to test whether a person was someone with whom I wanted to have a relationship, based on how they treated Phill.

Even now, I get twinges of embarrassment when someone looks at him askance when we're walking down the street or when I find myself over-explaining autism to acquaintances in an effort to soften their judgment of his behavior.

I know that some people are reading this and thinking: "Those experiences are no different from mine, and I don't have a sibling with autism." That may be true. As I said, all sibling relationships are complex, and certainly all of those relationships have benefits and drawbacks. A lot of what I experienced as a child may be a more concentrated version of what others go through as a sibling. I think, in general, that the experiences of people with siblings with autism are more intense, more prevalent, and last far later in life – often into adulthood.

Another issue that individuals who have siblings with typical development do not encounter is a role that I have always been aware of but am just now beginning to understand: I am going to be responsible for my brother in some way for the rest of my life.

Most people with a brother or sister with autism know from a very early age that a care taking role will be a part of their life, particularly if the typical sibling is the oldest. One of the reasons I need to tell my story – and Phill's story – is that I know how many brothers and sisters are out there, fully aware that at some point they will be their responsible for their brother too.

I first knew that this was going to be my role on some level when I was six years old. That was the year that Phill, who was three, learned how to talk. When he finally developed language, he had a serious speech impediment and was very difficult to understand. My mom and I understood him the best, as we spent the most time with him on a daily basis. But others, including my dad, had a very hard time deciphering what he was trying to say.

For many years after he gained speech, I was Phill's translator. This role was cemented after our parents divorced. When we visited our dad on weekends, I spoke for Phill the entire time. It was then I knew that Phill needed me in a way that other brothers did not seem to need their sisters, and that we would be linked in this way all of our lives. Although I will admit I didn't realize then how all encompassing that need might someday become.

Autism's Impact on Me

Phill's autism, obviously a major factor in his life, has influenced nearly every facet of mine as well. I tried to be a good daughter and a good student so my parents would be proud and not have to worry about me too. This is a role that many oldest children take on; I think that having a sibling with autism increases the pressure and the desire to be "good" and consequently, to be successful.

For me it wasn't about doing better than Phill or showing him up, but rather about trying to make life easier for my family by showing them they had nothing to worry about with me, allowing them to focus on Phill. It was a double-edged sword. Because it was neither my intention nor my desire to be better than Phill, I was often struck by overwhelming guilt every time I did succeed at something. I was terrified that Phill would feel as if he wasn't good enough, or that he would be upset because of what I accomplished. Still, those feelings never outweighed my drive to succeed and be "good".

I majored in psychology in college and earned a Masters in Social Work, in part because of my interest in how to make life easier for people like Phill and, in part, because of my fascination with how the mind works, all of which began with my curiosity about why Phill acted the way he did.

Some authors and researchers have found that siblings of people with disabilities are drawn to jobs in the social services fields. I am no exception. I have always worked in human services and I am drawn to learning more and focusing my work on disabilities – people with autism in particular — which is obviously due to having a brother who carries that label.

It's not clear why people who have siblings with disabilities often choose helping professions. Maybe it's because we are so used to helping others, and it feels like a natural fit. Maybe it's because we develop a greater sense of empathy than most people by seeing disability and the accompanying struggles close up. Or maybe it's because we have a better understanding that everyone can use a little help.

Phill and his autism also impacted who I dated, because how a man interacted with Phill was a major test for me about whether I would continue seeing him. All of the boys I dated seriously in high school and college were pretty good with Phill and had various levels of comfort with him. Most often, my long-term boyfriends established an uneasy truce. They never understood Phill very well, and were often a bit nervous about what he might do while they were around. Yet, they never spoke badly of him and they were very kind to him, which was my major concern in my younger years. There were certainly people in my life - kids in the neighborhood or at the pool, friends of friends, and kids in my classes — who would meet him and were not so nice.

One guy, who had known Phill for years (he was the friend of a longtime family friend) came up to me at a party and said, "God, your brother is really weird, isn't he?" I laughed off this comment because I know that Phill's odd behavior can sometimes make people uncomfortable. Also, at that stage in my life, I wasn't very good at confronting people who made statements about my brother. But this person didn't stop with one comment and continued to talk about Phill, analyzing each of his behaviors for their level of oddness. Eventually I told him off, and I have never forgiven that man for being such a totally insensitive jerk. I spend as little time in the same room with him as possible to this day. My close friends and boyfriends were always good to Phill.

When I started dating my ex-husband Karl, however, there was something different about his interactions with Phill. He didn't seem fearful of his behavior or freaked out that Phill might do something odd around him. He actually seemed to enjoy being with my brother and didn't mind doing things, just the two of them. This was something that had never happened with my other boyfriends. One of the many reasons I knew I wanted to marry Karl was that he and Phill really and truly bonded. This wasn't an effort that Karl undertook just to impress me, but his actual interest in getting to know Phill that drove their relationship. And while they didn't always get along - they could fight and annoy one another just like brothers - I knew their interactions and feelings were genuine and that is what was important to me.

Phill's diagnosis continues to impact my life in innumerable ways. I do not consider taking jobs that are outside of Washington State because I want to be close to my brother and my mom. I went to college 3,000 miles away from home and, at the time, thought I was leaving Washington for good. But the longer I was away, the more I was drawn back to both the state and my family. I moved back for graduate school, and it was then I fully realized I didn't want to live far away from my family again. The more I think about my brother's life and what we all want for him, and the role that I play in that life both for him and for my parents, the more convinced I am it is important for me to remain close by.

Before I married Karl, we discussed the responsibility I feel towards Phill and whether it was something my husband was willing to take on with me. He may have heard the old adage "you don't marry just me; you marry my family too", but he didn't realize how true that was in this case. I made it very clear to him I needed to plan for the possibility that Phill would need to live with me at some point during his life.

The Mantle of Responsibility

Having a sibling with autism is very different from having typically developing siblings. The most drastic difference is this feeling of responsibility for your sibling's future. Phill and I have a step-brother and step-sister with whom we are very close. While I am proud of their accomplishments and mourn their heartbreaks like any sibling, I do not feel as though I will some day be involved in every aspect of their day-to-day living. I am much more of an observer in their lives than I ever have been or ever will be in Phill's.

Traditional sibling relationships are centered on mutual emotional support and shared experiences. They are not focused on one sibling providing life-long care, support, and stability for the other. I think this is a fundamental difference and it inalterably changes the nature of the sibling relationship.

Sometimes the manifestation of that responsibility is unremarkable: acting like any other sister, checking in periodically to say hi, planning to spend time together to go to the movies or visit our grandpa –ways to stay connected to Phill and to give my parents a break.

Often, though, that responsibility is much more substantial. When my parents are older, or gone, my brother Phill is going to be my permanent responsibility. I will be the one to make sure he has a place to live, food to eat, a job or something with which to fill his days, and some semblance of enjoyment or happiness, if possible. I don't have to do this directly. I can find programs and pay to have someone else take care of the everyday details, but it will still be on my shoulders that he is looked after.

There are many similarities in experience among individuals who have a sibling with autism and those who have a sibling with another significant disability. Many of the emotions we feel are very much the same. But there are some major differences between autism and other disabilities that impact the relationship between the typical and the autistic siblings and which make the care taking responsibility even more challenging.

One of the most difficult aspects of helping someone with autism is the lack of social reciprocity. It is far easier for me to help a person when I feel that what I am doing is appreciated. With autism, that appreciation is hard to decipher. Phill is a very good-hearted person and I know he is grateful for the love and assistance he receives. However, I only learn that from emails he periodically sends to our parents and, on rare occasions, to me. He does not say "thank you" often. He rarely says "I love you", and he hates hugs and touching.

Another behavior that complicates the care taking relationship is the manner of social interaction that individuals with autism utilize. Instead of expressions of enjoyment or discussions of activities and common ground, most interactions with Phill are dominated by pointed and not-so-subtle comments about peccadilloes that most people would prefer no one noticed. In front of my boss one day Phill said, "You and Karl always fight. Like yesterday when you said..." and he repeated verbatim an entire silly argument my husband at the time and I had the night before. It was one of the many times that I wondered why I go out of my way to include him in things when he seems committed to embarrass me or hurt my feelings.

It was also a major issue between my husband and me before we divorced. Whenever Phill started picking on some aspect of my character or something stupid that I had done, Karl would get upset. Usually he and Phill got along well, but during these times he would snap at Phill and expresses his frustration by suggesting that we not help Phill anymore if he was going to take us (and me in particular) for granted. This made me defensive of Phill, even though I did not appreciate this behavior either.

Then comes the perennial argument of whether a particular behavior is something he has control over or whether it is part of his autism. If Phill were blind and he walked into a table and knocked over my favorite lamp, no one would ever say they should stop inviting him to the house. But Phill saying something potentially hurtful because of his autism is much harder to understand, and therefore much harder to forgive. Autism makes the job of caring for someone else much larger because it feels like a thankless job and because it can engender so much resentfulness in the caretaker.

Similarly, the close relationship that many brothers and sisters and even many typical and disabled brothers and sisters have is not the same as the relationship that exists between a typical sibling and an autistic sibling. There is a barrier that cannot be permeated. In my relationship with Phill, it is the fact that I cannot talk about real feelings with him. It makes him uncomfortable; he does everything in his power to change the subject, usually opting to become surly and loud instead of engaging in the conversation.

Phill has a hard time feeling empathy for other people, especially if someone is sad or upset. This isn't always a symptom of autism, but it is in Phill's case, and it makes it hard to be close to him. There is no comfort in sharing what you are experiencing because he does not respond with consoling words or gestures; he is silent, changes the subject, or tries to top whatever you are describing with something he has experienced that he perceives as much worse. "Yes, but it is worse/hardest/best for me because..." is the beginning of every other sentence with Phill.

Instead of hearing his concerns for his own life or his feelings of success, the language he uses and his need to top everything creates an environment of competition and sometimes invites bickering about who has it worst or best or the most. When I take a step back from myself in these moments, I am embarrassed I am arguing with my autistic brother about such ridiculous things – like who is colder when we are skiing. Yet that is my reaction to constantly being told my experience is not as intense as his own.

One challenge in the care taking role that doesn't have anything to do with the person with autism is the availability of services to support the caregiver. For some disabilities, there is a system of services set up to assist families. With most, however, those services are much less prevalent than one would hope, particularly for adults.

For families dealing with autism, part of the issue is that there is not one type of autism or one example of a person with autism. People with autism have a plethora of skills and deficits, and every autistic person needs different kinds of help.

For children with autism there are more interventions, programs, and services that can help to mitigate their symptoms and assist them with school completion. At last, a real understanding of the disorder is beginning to break through, along with services that can help children succeed both in life and in controlling and overcoming the disability. But there is far less awareness, and thus far fewer services, for adults with autism and, in general, for adults with disabilities.

Taking care of a person with autism is a responsibility fraught with difficulties, and the lack of services and places to turn for help simply exacerbates an already confusing and frightening job. Phill needs help finding a vocation and learning skills that are necessary to perform well in that profession. He can do a job with great proficiency and gusto once given the tools to accomplish it, and when an employer is either able to get past his quirky behavior or he is able to present himself in a more professional manner during the interview process.

Phill wants friends and a girlfriend, but he does not know how to get them; he needs assistance learning social skills and places to be with people his own age. He also wants to live on his own, but he is very susceptible to negative influences.

As the people who want to keep Phill safe, we as his family have to ask: where can he be on his own and still be safe? Does he need to live with someone in the family? What about finding an apartment nearby? Is there some kind of facility where he could live on his own but have someone check-in on him, or where others like him might live as well? These are some of the issues with which my family and I struggle. There do not appear to be answers or services readily available for people like Phill.

I don't think of the inevitability of my responsibility for Phill as a burden. It is what it is; it is what my life has always been and is always going to be. Regardless of how you view it, there are feelings that go along with being the typical sibling that never get talked about, and are rarely acknowledged, even by the person experiencing them. These emotions are important to recognize — and accept — because they impact the sibling relationship and will have an effect on your ability to take care of your brother or sister.

THE GOOD FEELINGS

I believe one of the hardest things, and one of the most important things, to consider for those of us who have a sibling with autism is how to separate how we feel about that brother or sister from how we feel about autism itself. It isn't just important to think about those emotions, but also to discuss and express them as best we can.

I'm not suggesting that you wallow in the bad feelings or to try to mask the difficult experiences in order to focus on the good ones. It's necessary to embrace and accept that all of those feelings are real, acceptable, and understandable.

If we try to pretend that we do not feel angry or jealous or guilty or frustrated, we are not being honest with ourselves, and we are creating an even larger barrier between ourselves and our siblings with autism – not to mention lying to ourselves. In most cases, an autistic brother or sister is not going to say "Gee, it looks like something is wrong. What's going on with you right now?" Not in the way that other friends and family might say.

That is part of the autism itself. Most people with autism do not look beyond what is plainly evident on the surface. That means that if we are not acknowledging our emotions in that relationship, no one is.

It took me a long time to realize that when I was not owning my own emotional responses, my relationship with my brother suffered, my relationship with my family suffered, and my ability to care for myself suffered.

Now, regardless of how difficult it might be to express my anger or frustration, I know I have to if I am to be a fully functioning, caring, involved person. Once, when someone told me "You have to take care of yourself in order to care for others", I thought that seemed selfish. I felt as if that was an excuse to do for myself instead of for my brother, a justification for not staying focused on him and his needs.

Now I get it. I'm not doing a good job for anyone else if I am pushing aside my own feelings and needs. When I do that, I don't function as well; I start doing things on automatic, but I'm not as invested or involved as I should be. That isn't healthy, and it isn't helpful. Taking care of ourselves can be as simple as talking to friends about our frustrations or soaking in a long bath.

I usually need a short time off by myself. I'll take a walk, go to the movies, or get a massage - by myself. Sometimes I limit my time with Phill. He typically spends two nights a week at my house, but during those times when I am feeling burdened or annoyed I'll say, "This week I'm going to pick you up Monday morning" instead of having him over Sunday night, and he doesn't seem to mind.

What I have finally come to terms with is that I'm not a saint. What? You can't believe it? Well, it's true. And that means that sometimes - actually, relatively often - I can't be all things to all people. I guess that everyone, myself included, will just have to live with that.

There are a lot of emotions that we will experience in our lifetimes, both related to our siblings and in other arenas of life. The feelings I describe here are those I have experienced most often with my brother. But my feelings are by no means the "right" ones or the only ones. There are no right or wrong responses to autism or to interactions with our own siblings.

Some of these emotions are the most common, and you may not have any experience with them, or you may be more familiar with different emotions that I don't even touch on. I illustrate my feelings only to suggest that there are many that we often pretend we don't have or sweep away, which makes it hard for us to be honest with ourselves.

These are some of mine - the good ones — some that I have embraced and some that I am still grappling with every day.

Love

It all starts with love. I love my family. I love being close to them and knowing we will always be there for each other. I love spending time with them and sharing holidays; I love fighting over where to go for dinner and laughing about nothing in particular.

My love for my brother is one of the primary reasons I do not resent, most days, the inevitability of my role as caretaker. My love for Phill conquers everything else and makes it so that I cannot imagine my life without him, nor would I want to.

Love is what is going to carry us through as our brothers' and sisters' keepers and help us avoid killing them in the process. This is the feeling that we all must come back to as we deal with the difficult, annoying or challenging parts of having an autistic sibling. Love is what drives my parents to be stubborn and difficult about where my brother should live in the future – their love for him and their love for me and their desire for us both to live as independently and happily as possible.

Love is what helps me accept that Phill doesn't want to hug me ever or to say "I love you" out loud. It is also what ensures that he always knows just what to get me for my birthday and to remember every little thing that I like and dislike.

Love is the single biggest reason that I know I will always be there for my brother, no matter what he needs, and it is also one of the feelings that I must closely monitor – so that I don't do things that are detrimental to myself in a misguided effort to honor my love for my brother.

Humor

Phill and I have a very good relationship. We have great times together. We have similar senses of humor, and we can make each other laugh like no one else. When I was thinking about the good feelings, one of the first that popped into my mind was silliness. Phill and I are goofy and silly and, though we can irritate each other in a way no one else can, we also entertain each other for hours with quirky, stupid humor that only we find entertaining.

When Phill started volunteering at my office, we often drove home through the dark, in rainy rush hour traffic that is a regular occurrence for Seattle commuters. As I'd grow tense and frustrated with traffic, carpool lane or not, Phill would almost immediately doze off, which I found totally and completely infuriating.

Out of exasperation one night, I poked him in the leg, causing him to jump about three feet in surprise. "What was that for?" he demanded. To which I replied, "If I can't sleep, neither can you." As payback, Phill spent the rest of the ride pretending to fall asleep. Each time his head lolled forward, I poked him in the leg with my index finger. While I think we both started out with the intention of annoying the other, this grew into a game that has not gotten old more than six months later. Now, almost every drive home, at some point, Phill pretends to be asleep and I poke him and startle him. This game is totally pointless and makes no sense, but it makes us laugh every time for some ridiculous reason.

There isn't anyone else who I can joke with like that – being as silly as I want to be – other than Phill. It is something that I am very grateful for in our relationship. It is also a "normal" feeling; other brothers and sisters have similar bonds where they just "get" one another's humor and can enjoy each other in this way.

When Phill and I are being goofy, I feel like we can forget about the autism for a while, which is such a relief. Thinking about the impacts of autism all the time is exhausting, even if it is in the back of our minds, and we both revel in the release. It is exhausting to monitor Phill's behavior, to worry about the future, to consider what he can and can't do in a given situation. I'm sure it's exhausting for Phill too – trying to control all of the quirks that might annoy someone without being entirely sure what it is that sets people off. It is draining on all of our relationships too – with each other, with our parents and with others. Having the opportunity to laugh and let our hair down is an important tool for escaping the burden for a little while.

The silliness and sense of humor also breaks up tension. Some of the manifestations of Phill's autism can be so distracting and frustrating that I know I often snap at him even when I know much of the behavior is out of his control. His sense of humor and our ability to laugh together brings the stress level down significantly and can help remind me to avoid taking things so personally and to give him a break.

Loyalty

I have always felt an intense loyalty to my brother, as I'm sure many other siblings feel towards their brothers and sisters, whether or not they have autism. While it is possible to feel burdened by a sense of loyalty, for me it is something to cherish. Loyalty fills my heart with fire; it makes me passionate about protecting and promoting my siblings. The loyalty I feel towards Phill is part of what assures me that I can and will care for him after our parents are gone. To take on that great responsibility is due in part to our ties as siblings and the loyalty I have to him and to that bond.

Loyalty is also what helps me avoid embarrassment about his behavior. My loyalty to my brother trumps my concern about what other people think. And honestly, I am grateful to have something that reminds me that it doesn't matter what others think.

Instead of hanging my head in shame during an episode when we attended the Festival of Trees – a fundraiser for the local children's hospital where decorated Christmas trees are auctioned off to the highest bidder – my loyalty allowed me to rise above other people's judgement. When a stranger walking behind us commented to her partner that Phill was talking loudly, I started talking louder myself. Phill wasn't being out of line, first of all. He was speaking a little louder than some of the people around us, but it was very cacophonous in the events center and hard to hear when you were having a conversation. More importantly, he had every right to talk – even if it was a little louder than this woman would have preferred. Therefore, when I raised my voice, I also commented that some people had to learn to be more polite. I have to say that being loyal to Phill in that instance felt far better than being embarrassed that he was bothering someone.

Loyalty helps us to stand up against the world, united as a team. When relatives invited me to their house for Thanksgiving, but didn't invite Phill, my loyalty to my brother made me turn down the offer. However, it didn't feel like a sacrifice, it felt like Phill and I were in this thing together, and I knew, had the situation been reversed, he would have done the same for me. That is an important feeling; It helps remove some of the isolation and eases that feeling that I am doing this all alone.

But loyalty is also a dangerous feeling. It can blind a person to the real needs of their sibling – what might be best for them – in a misguided belief that just because you care and maybe care even more than anyone else, that you are the only one who knows what the right thing is for your brother or sister.

I have a vision of what I would like my brother's life to be like, what I think he should and shouldn't do, be exposed to, experience. He doesn't necessarily agree with me, and I have to be careful not to misinterpret my own loyalty and concern for what is best for him.

Sometimes people have to learn through mistakes – or experiences. Things that I believe are mistakes may not be wrong for Phill. I need to give him room to have power over of his own life, and I need to be careful not to try to control his life too much.

I also have to remind myself that his wanting to spread his wings and live his own life is not him being disloyal to me. We are in this together, but we are two independent, strong-willed people, which is to be respected, not resented. In that same vein, I have to watch my loyalty and not presume that just because I want to respect Phill's wishes and honor our bond by allowing him his independence, I can let him do whatever pops into his head. It is a fine balance, as with much of our relationship, and it is hard to walk that line much of the time.

Joy

My relationship with my brother does bring me a considerable amount of joy, though I often don't remember that until I am reflecting on our time together. He is great fun to be with. He does particularly well in one-on-one situations, and we have had numerous good talks, fun excursions, and memorable times together.

A few years ago we went to a huge craft fair for the holidays. I was considering selling some crafts and wanted to get some ideas about display and marketing, but no one really wanted to go with me except for Phill. I told Phill why I was there and the types of things I was looking for, and he became an invaluable help and a fun companion for the fair.

We found things to show each other; he made notes in his notebook for me about ideas and prices; and we walked the aisles as people who enjoy spending time together, not as someone with autism and his sister. We have a lot of experiences like that which are very special, and the key is to remember them – not years down the road, but in the moment. That isn't an easy thing to accomplish – we all struggle to live in the moment.

The best advice I have for how to live in the moment is to let go of caring what everyone around you is thinking or saying about you and your sibling. When you have an inkling that you are experiencing one of those times that you want to remember, stop and savor it. Stand still. Stop talking. Absorb the sights and sounds, even if only for a second. Allowing yourself those moments is important because it reminds you why it is nice to have your brother or sister in your life in the first place.

I also get a lot of joy from watching him find enjoyment in things on his own. He has always loved to draw and create jewelry. I love seeing his newest creations and imaginings. He has been very focused on motorcycles for the last few years and recently decided to start drawing them – designing them, I should say. For Christmas I got him some good pencils and sketchpads and a book on drawing Choppers. He brings those tools to my house now every week when he stays over; while I work on whatever project I have on hand, he draws, pausing every now and then to show me how it has progressed. I love watching him succeed and be rewarded for his persistence instead of being chided for it. Any time he is able to channel his considerable energy and focus into a project and make something out of it, my heart swells.

One of the things that brings me the most joy is his pride in his job at my office. For a couple of years, Phill has worked at my office two days a week. He started out as a volunteer until eventually my generous boss found a way to pay him. At first I think he saw it as something to get him out of the house and a way to help me out, which he is always willing to do. But as he saw that we had real stuff for him to do, I think it grew into much more.

Aside from general office assistant tasks like getting the mail, sending out packages and the like, he has been compiling a database of articles for me that now includes 2,500 documents with titles, authors, publishers, dates, and other pertinent details. He developed a strong sense of ownership for the job. He tells me how much I need him in order to do my own job, and relates — with a sense of glee — that he can't miss a day when he is scheduled because our boss wants him to be there. The feeling that he belongs and is giving back to the world makes him happy, which in turn makes me proud. He's skilled at the job, a hard worker, and a real asset to our agency.

I am often delighted by the little things he remembers and shares, things that demonstrate how much he cares for me. He recently made me a CD comprised of songs he remembered that I loved or thought I would enjoy. It is a great mix, and virtually every song puts a smile on my face because I remember or guess why it made him think of me. He included music from movies we've seen together and songs we called "company music" because our dad always played them when our parents were hosting a dinner party when we were little.

It is touching to know he remembers things that matter to me, especially when so often it feels as if he can only think of himself. While his uncanny ability to remember every word and conversation I have ever uttered or engaged in can be a very trying trait in many situations, it also makes Phill an excellent gift giver. Months before a holiday, he catalogs in his head things that I want or need, then divides them among family members to ensure that I get all of the things I might desire.

I don't want to overstate those feelings of joy or to use them to cover up the more difficult emotions, but it is imperative to remember why I want to care for my brother, and these simple moments are some of my reasons.

I like being an integral part of my brother's life. I love seeing him excel or even just try something new. And I honestly enjoy him as a person. It isn't the guilt or the responsibility or the need that drive me to want to care for my brother. It is the simple fact that he is my brother, and I enjoy him and want him to be happy.

Being Needed

It feels rather selfish to say so, but the fact that Phill needs me is one of the good feelings I associate with our relationship. It feels selfish because it seems like I want Phill to need help so I can feel special. I like being needed.

I like having a purpose and being able to help and feeling important because I fill that role. I don't think there is anything wrong with appreciating being needed, so long as I continue to be aware that being needed is part of what drives what I am doing. I would hate to find myself encouraging Phill to lean on me more than he has to so that I could be his savior - although it is easy for both of us to use his autism as an excuse for me to do things for him.

When we were children and I translated what he was saying for other people, that feeling of being needed was very strong. As Phill's speech started to improve, I continued to speak for him on a regular basis, both because it was habit and I felt he needed me to. One day my step-mom took me aside and said, "You have to try and let Phill speak for himself. Let people work out what he is trying to say. If he doesn't learn to make an effort to be understood and people don't try to understand him, what will happen when you aren't around? How will he communicate?"

This felt hurtful to me at the time. I felt as if she was saying I was doing something bad when all I was trying to do was help. But I did take pains not to interpret everything he said and let others, my dad in particular, figure out for themselves what he was saying. And she was right. He found a way to have his needs met. Although it often took more than one repetition to understand what he was saying, what he wanted or needed, through trial and error, my dad and others found ways to communicate with him. I had to control my own desire to be needed and let his independence take precedence over that emotion. I continue to struggle with that balance to this day.

Hope

When I see Phill succeed at a task or in a particular role, I feel an immense sense of hope. I hope he has found something he can be passionate about, that he can succeed at on a regular basis. I hope he is on a path to find a place for himself in a world that is rarely tolerant of people like him. I hope he is leading the way for other people like him, so that those following in his footsteps don't have to struggle so hard. I hope things are going to be easier for our whole family.

Hope is sometimes a scary feeling, though. It feels like a very thin line between having hope for him and his aspirations and expecting too much, only to be disappointed later. At the same time, I don't want to expect too little - to lose that hope - and force him to achieve less because I didn't believe in him enough or give him room to try.

Hope is also an incredibly tricky emotion within a family dynamic because we don't all feel it at the same time or about the same things.

As a family, we have to be careful not to suck the hope out of our own or each others visions for Phill's future as we plan ahead and talk about what our roles will be in the future. Most importantly I want to ensure that Phill continues to have hope, because without that, what reason does he have to even try?

None of us knows what he is capable of, or how accommodations might be found for him to be able to achieve his dreams. The world, and the United States in particular, becomes more aware and knowledgeable about autism everyday. As that happens, more services, more research, and more opportunities become available. As caretakers responsible for a person with autism, we have to think about all of the possibilities - all of the "what ifs". But just because we have backup plans and contingencies does not mean we have to stop believing and hoping that our siblings will achieve all their heart's desires. I believe the minute we give up on hope, they will too.

Pride

I often have a sense of amazement, astonishment, and pride when I think about all that Phill has experienced up to now in his relatively short life. I don't know that I could keep pushing through if I were in his shoes. The constant struggle to accomplish everyday tasks — always being told to be quiet or to stop or start doing something, lacking friends and independence, the astonishing frustration present every day — I don't know if I could stand to face it day in and day out. But Phill continues to push forward, accomplishing new things and finding new ways of being that are truly amazing.

He certainly gets down about his life on occasion. But for the most part, he is positive and happily tackles the new challenges with which he is presented each day. I'm often awestruck by the ways he compensates for things he's not good at. He rarely reaches goals in traditional ways; he takes a circuitous and time-consuming route, but he is often successful. I experience a great sense of wonder at his ability and perseverance. I garner strength from watching him. I often find myself thinking, "Well, if Phill can do that, I ought to be able to do this." He can be very inspiring. I don't think that most people are blessed to have an inspiration like this in their everyday lives.

When I think of all that my brother has overcome, all that he has accomplished in spite of his autism, I am extremely proud of him. The most impressive trait that Phill has is his unwavering belief in the good that exists in this world. I think that if I had been exposed to as many barriers as he has met in his journey through life, I would be a cynical, pessimistic person. I would not try anything. I would just assume it was going to be too hard.

That is not Phill's way at all. He believes in himself, but more importantly, he does the things that he likes because he wants to. It does not matter to him how they will turn out or whether they will meet other people's standards of "good" or not. He makes an effort to overcome obstacles that most people do not even consider every day. For the most part, throughout it all, he keeps his sense of humor and his unique and honest view of the world intact.

Pride is an important emotion in our relationships with our siblings because it helps us preserve our hope and desires for their future when we see them succeed. Each time we feel proud of an accomplishment, it is an inspiration and incentive to see them succeed again and accomplish even more. It is a feeling that helps ward off the fatigue and doubt that can plague our efforts.

Gratitude

Finally, I am grateful for my brother. I am grateful both to simply have him in my life, and for what he is able to teach me. He has made me more tolerant, more accepting, more patient (though he says I'm still not all that patient), and a better person. I'm also grateful for my time with my brother. I'm happy he allows me to help him, that he wants to spend time with me, and that he trusts me.

I'm grateful for our good times together. I'm grateful I do not currently need to have Phill live with me. I'm grateful that my father has the resources so that Phill does not need to have a high-paying job in order to be taken care of, and that I do not need to worry about depriving myself or my future family in order to make sure that Phill's needs are met.

Another thing I am grateful for is a bit more difficult to talk about. It took me a long time to admit it to myself, but I am grateful that I am not the one with autism. Is that a difficult thing to say? Absolutely. Is it wrong? No. I am grateful I don't have autism. I am glad I know how to read people's emotions. I am so thankful that I did not have to struggle the way that Phill did in school, that I made friends, and had relationships. But I'm ashamed of myself for feeling grateful about it. Everyone has the "why him and not me" reaction to things. When your child has a car accident, when your wife gets sick, when your loved ones experience pain, it is often our reaction to say, "Why couldn't it have happened to me instead?" or "Why did it happen to them?" But I'm not saying, "Why couldn't it have happened to me instead?" The guilt comes from feeling grateful for that.

I do believe, however, that I am in Phill's life for a reason – to help him, to guide him, to watch out for him. I have come to pacify myself with the thought that it wasn't me for a good reason. But that isn't necessarily the case.

The truth is simple. Phill has autism and I don't, and I'm happy that I don't have it. It's a fact, and it is something I need to come to terms with and accept. That is the first of many of the not-so-good feelings that need to be acknowledged when you have a sibling who has autism.

THE NOT-SO-GOOD FEELINGS

It is much harder for the typical sibling to own the socially unacceptable, negative, or "bad" feelings we have about our autistic siblings and the reality of our situations than it is to accept the good feelings. No one wants to admit that sometimes we feel jealous, angry, guilty, and embarrassed.

I always wanted to be the good kid. I tried to save my parents any problems; the worst thing I could imagine was letting my mom and dad know that I was unhappy or annoyed because my brother was different. Even as I entered adulthood, the politically correct world I generally inhabit made it almost impossible to admit that having a sibling with autism was sometimes uncomfortable, frustrating, and – God forbid – something I would rather not have in my life. The only thing I felt comfortable saying was that the challenges my brother and my family had faced made me the person I am, and I am grateful for that. That is not an overstatement; I am grateful for my brother and for the lessons I have learned because of his autism.

Still, that is not anywhere close to the full story of what it feels like to have an autistic sibling. What I am learning now is to accept in my own heart and mind those feelings that are not-so-good, and that I have to talk about them. If I don't, I am not being honest with myself nor anyone around me. That isn't to say I need to make my brother or my parents feel bad, or that it is always difficult having a brother with autism. But I don't believe I can be a good sister or care for anyone, myself or my brother, by pretending there are never any down sides to living with autism.

Guilt

When discussing the good feelings, I mentioned being grateful I was not the one born with autism. But admitting feeling grateful for being "typical" is a slippery slope, and it leads very easily into the dominant not-so-good feeling that, at least for me, is a constant, ever-present entity in my life: Guilt.

Guilt is the inescapable, universal, inevitable feeling that exists for those of us with siblings with autism. It is big and little, in understandable situations and in seemingly innocuous ones.

One New Year's Eve my brother called, having overheard a conversation about what I was doing for the evening, and asked if he could come to the party too. I did not want him to come, because I would have to be responsible for him all evening. Sometimes at parties he is totally appropriate; other times he is loudly inappropriate and embarrassing. I never know which Phill I am going to get. Plus this was a party that included people I didn't know. It's one thing to take Phill places where everyone knows him and knows about his autism. It is a whole different thing to take him someplace where he will be looked at askance all night by virtual strangers. I didn't want to spend New Year's Eve watching after my brother, explaining his behavior to friends and acquaintances. I just wanted to let go and have a good time.

After I got off the phone with my brother, I burst into tears. I didn't want him to go with us, but I felt guilty about not wanting to hang out with him. Where else was he going to go for New Year's? He didn't want to hang out with our parents any more than any 22-year-old would, and he didn't have any friends of his own to spend time with. Eventually I pulled myself together and called Phill back and took him to the party. It turned out we had a really good time. But I feel that guilt every time I am invited to an event or somewhere that Phill would enjoy.

I don't know what to do about the guilt besides accept it exists. I can't think of any way to stop feeling it. At this point, it is a part of who I am. It can be a good reminder not to take myself or my problems too seriously, and to think about the needs of others. But it is imperative it not take over my life, nor sap the enjoyment from the things I accomplish and love.

Guilt may always be there, but it is ok to say, "This is a stupid thing to feel guilty about." It is ok to be proud of yourself and your accomplishments. It is ok to take time for yourself. It's ok to go to a party without your brother. It is ok to put yourself first. Those are the things I try to remember. Because if I let the guilt take over, I'm not going to be a happy person. If I am not taking care of myself and my own needs to make myself happy, I don't think I'm going to be a very good role model for my brother. Nor will I be able to help him find out how to make himself happy.

Anger

Another common emotion is anger. Sometimes I feel so very angry I can barely contain myself. Sometimes I am angry at Phill – for not doing what I want him to do, for being annoying, for antagonizing my mom, my step-dad or me, either on purpose or inadvertently, until everyone is so aggravated with each other, we are barely speaking.

Sometimes I am angry at my parents – for not having him properly diagnosed sooner so he could have received more services, for not planning better for the future so I would know what to expect, for not trying hard enough, or for not paying enough attention to me.

Sometimes I'm angry at God — for making Phill autistic, for letting this happen to my family when there are so many bad people in the world who deserve to have bad things happen to them, for doing this to Phill and not letting him have an easier life.

And sometimes I'm angry at the world - incensed that society isn't more accepting of people who are different, that there aren't more services and supports for people like Phill. I'm especially irritated with those individuals who have every opportunity handed to them, then squander it while Phill struggles; and I'm upset with those who think that we, as a society, shouldn't try to make life better for people like Phill and others who are less fortunate than ourselves because it doesn't impact them directly.

In some ways, anger is one of the best feelings because it seems so tangible. There are people or systems to be angry at, which feels so much better than being sad or scared and having no direction for the emotions. Anger can incite change. When I'm angry I'm more likely to tell people how I feel, more likely to advocate for services for Phill or changes to our systems, or to talk to my parents about what we are going to do.

But anger is also one of the worst feelings. I don't want to be angry at my family or my brother or the world; being angry in and of itself doesn't solve anything or make anything better. It just drains me and makes me feel bad in the end.

Anger often circles back to guilt, creating a vicious cycle. If I am angry at my brother for talking incessantly and interrupting a conversation and I snap at him, I often end up feeling bad for being so rough on him. Then I feel guilty because I know the interrupting is linked to his autism and I should be able to be more patient.

The best way to deal with the anger is to acknowledge it and let it go. If the anger is justified and it results in a change in a situation, then I use it. If it is irrational or without purpose, the best thing is to say, "Gee, that really infuriates me," and move on. Holding onto the anger is too time consuming and can create a wall of resentment and frustration that doesn't do any good.

However, if I don't let myself feel the anger, at least for a little while, it simmers inside me and I can't let it go. Being angry is normal. But unless I recognize it and accept it, I risk having it boil up and spill out when I least expect it.

Embarrassment

As a child and especially as a teenager, embarrassment rivaled guilt for its prevalence in my life. Most often I was embarrassed by Phill's outfits. But his behavior and statements could also bring up an embarrassed reaction quickly.

The times when he insisted on coming to my school functions wearing his Superman shirt (with cape) or the furry hands from his Teen Wolf outfit were bad. Almost worse, in my mind, were when his outfit was odd, but not really related to an identifiable character. For a while when he was about ten, he wore one white golfing glove with most of his outfits, along with about six necklaces at any one time. Those were the times when I could tell people weren't just thinking "Hey, that kid really likes Superman," but rather "What is the deal with that kid?"

I thought I would grow out of feeling embarrassment as an adult. I didn't. I am embarrassed by the things Phill does and says all the time, even now. Luckily, I have mostly gotten over caring what other people think about how he is dressed. There are people who are wearing far stranger outfits in the world these days, and I don't have time to care if someone thinks what Phill is wearing is weird.

The same cannot be said for his behavior and conversations. One such example is when we were walking with our boss and Phill started walking with one stiff leg and one normal leg. He swung the stiff leg around as he walked as if it was in a cast. Another time he will randomly start walking in an exaggerated march with his knees practically slamming into his chin as he soldiers down the street. And while those actions cause flashes of embarrassment and discomfort, they pale in comparison to the personal stories and inappropriate comments that Phill uses to participate in conversation. Those are the times when my cheeks flush a bright pink, I sink down low in my chair, and I wish I were anywhere else.

What is there to do about embarrassments like these? Not allow him to talk – ever? Not take him out where someone I know might be? These aren't reasonable options. So I'm stuck with feeling embarrassed and often on edge whenever he opens his mouth or walks down the street. It is an extremely draining and frustrating way to feel.

Recently I learned from my co-workers that sometimes I overreact and am embarrassed unnecessarily. Especially with people who are used to Phill and know what to expect from him, the things he says and does can be entertaining or a curiosity. He isn't reflecting on me – he's his own person. I'm learning that what I see as a sister that makes me cringe, isn't as big a deal as I make it out to be.

I'm finding out that the best way to deal with embarrassment is to consider whether something really is embarrassing, or whether I am just being oversensitive. I've found that being aware that the people we spend time with aren't sitting around saying, "Wow, what a weirdo," has reduced my feelings of embarrassment.

Realizing that many people can accept Phill for who he is, the same way they accept me, decreases the amount of time I spend feeling embarrassed. It also helps me let my brother just be himself, instead of constantly feeling like I need to control his every move.

Sadness

When I think about Phill's life, I feel a lot of sadness. I try not to dwell on it, and I hope I don't share or show that sadness to Phill, because he is doing the very best he can. For the most part, I think he is happy with his life; I respect that. I want him to be happy and I don't want to draw attention to things he might not otherwise think about.

Yet, when I consider how much he has always wanted his own friends, and now more than anything, a girlfriend, I feel a lump in my stomach. Those things seem so out of reach for him. I hate that – I hate that I can't figure out a way to put them within his grasp. The same is true for many of his dreams – like moving to San Francisco and getting a great job. I don't know those things won't happen, but I know it will be very difficult for Phill to acquire them. The unfairness of it all and my total inability to make it better makes me incredibly sad.

Sadness often arises from those feelings of guilt and embarrassment as well. I feel a little sad and sorry for myself on occasion when I am exhausted by the guilt of considering Phill's feelings for every outing I take. I feel badly he can't make things happen for himself to both give him a sense of autonomy and relieve some of the pressure I put on myself to always consider his needs.

Then, too, I feel a sense of sadness when I am embarrassed by the things he says and does because I know he doesn't set out to be odd, or intend to be weird, and he doesn't know any better than I do how to stop.

Dealing with the sadness isn't easy. As with all of these feelings, it isn't an easy thing to think about. Since much of it comes from things we know we can't change, it is accompanied by a big dose of helplessness. Most of the time I remember the many good things in Phill's life, and in my life, and that it is a waste to dwell on things that might never be.

When I get a wave of sadness, I try to turn it around and think about what we do have, and how fortunate we have been in so many ways, even if some things are not as we might have chosen. I try to find something I can change or do to combat feeling sad and helpless – maybe taking Phill to the movies or going on a walk – to be reminded of the things we have to be happy about.

When I just need to be sad, or when I'm sad for something real, instead of what might have been, I give myself permission to feel it. Sometimes I let myself cry, because it can be so cleansing and such a relief. I think it's important to give myself time to feel sad, because then I can move on and feel better.

Loss

A feeling that accompanies sadness is a tremendous feeling of loss. As we grow into adults, it becomes clear to me we are not going to have the same kind of bond as other brothers and sisters. The relationship that some siblings have is a friendship based not only on shared experiences but also on an enjoyment of one another's company and the appreciation of what the other has experienced in life — how they feel, when they need support and when they need to laugh.

I feel an intense loss knowing I may never feel that kind of closeness with Phill. There is something about the difference between our developmental levels that makes a relationship like that impossible.

Recently I have grown much closer to our step-brother and step-sister. While I cherish these relationships and am grateful for them, I find I feel an intense amount of guilt and sadness about feeling close to them, in a way I cannot, and do not feel close to Phill.

I am the most torn about my relationship with my step-brother, probably because he is a boy and lives close by, and we can talk about what is really happening in our lives and how we feel. I wish I didn't want the relationship be strong. Knowing what a relationship with a brother can be like and not being able to attain it with Phillip, whom I love so much, solidifies that sense of loss in me.

I regret the loss I suspect others experience as well. I don't think anyone in our family has the relationship they might have wished for with Phillip, and I think that is incredibly sad, for him and for us. It isn't just the autism itself that impedes our relationships, either. It is also our unyielding and often unconscious need to constantly parent and teach Phill – to modify his behavior. It is our reaction to Phill's autism and our belief about how we should behave (in order to get him to behave the way we feel is appropriate) that inserts itself in our ability to just be with him.

I can't help feeling a sometimes overpowering sense of loss for his – and my – potential. For him, I feel as if we missed an opportunity to get him the right services at a young age, when research has shown the greatest gains can be made. At the same time, I don't believe the "right" services existed, or even exist today for my brother.

Phill received a lot of help as a kid, which is part of the reason he is as high-functioning as he is now. But what he didn't have when he was young were services that were better crafted to impact the type of autism he had. I often wonder if we somehow did a disservice to him by not getting him diagnosed sooner, and if, because of that, he has missed out on experiences and chances for more in his life. This can be a useless thing to ponder, because my parents took him to countless doctors and got the diagnoses available at the time; there was little understanding of "high-functioning autism" in America twenty-five years ago. In fact, at that time, the label of autism was as much a hindrance as it was a useful tool. So maybe Phill is better off now that he might have been. Even so, I can't help but wonder how life would have been different had the autism diagnosis been made earlier, and that instills a sense of loss in me.

At the same time, I wonder if because of his autism I have held myself back. Did I use it as a reason, real or not, to come home to go to graduate school instead of going to New York or somewhere else? Have I made choices based on his needs that inadvertently denied me the opportunity to live my life to its fullest? I have a friend from college who is living in London while her family is in Pennsylvania. Would I live in London if my brother didn't have autism?

I sometimes feel as if I missed out on things because of my sense of duty to my brother, and that certainly feels like a loss even when it doesn't feel like a sacrifice. However, if it weren't autism or Phill, I would have made choices based on some other factors. Each of us makes decisions throughout our lives and wonder about what would have happened had we made another choice. We all have tipping points – events, experiences, people or moments — that can be a deciding factor in the choices we make.

Autism was certainly a factor for me. Was it the only factor? No. Was it the deciding factor? I don't know. I think it would have been unhealthy had I based entire decisions on Phill and his autism. That would have created too much resentment and anger. My life still needs to be my life, or I wouldn't be any use to either of us. I don't think I regret the choices I have made, but I do wonder about and mourn the path not taken and wonder how my life will be impacted in the future.

Those feelings of loss are inherently focused on the past. The only way I have found to deal with them is to recognize them, and to make plans for the future with an awareness of the impact those not-so-good emotions have had on my life up to now.

That's not to say I make every move based on whether I think I will feel sadness or loss. That kind of thinking could lead to a paralyzing state of indecisiveness. We always give up something when we make a choice. But weighing the choices with a realistic view of the future and a clear understanding of the past helps ensure making the best decision possible.

Jealousy

Jealousy is a very tricky business when you have a brother or sister with autism. It seems to lead directly to guilt if you feel jealous of someone who has so many struggles in all the other parts of life. But it happens.

My jealousy flares when my brother, who works two days a week and has five days of unscheduled time, talks about what time he wakes up in the morning - or should I say afternoon.

Jealousy has existed for years in relation to the time he spends with our mom and regarding the things I perceive he "gets away with" because of his autism. When I was little, my jealousy was typical. It didn't occur to me to feel bad about being jealous of Phill; I felt it when he got things I didn't — a trip somewhere, the front seat of the car, birthday presents — the normal stuff. Feeling bad about the jealousy didn't occur until high school and college, when I started to be more aware of Phill's autism and thought about the differences between what I was able to do and have in my life versus what he had. I definitely still get jealous, but now it's often accompanied by that perennial feeling of guilt. I try to stop the cycle to guilt from occurring, because I think jealousy can be healthy when it doesn't spiral down into the bottomless pit of guilt.

It is healthy for me to want something Phill has or to be like Phill every now and then, and I think it is good for Phill to know he has things or experiences other people wish for. Conversely, I think jealousy is good for both of us in that sometimes Phill can use a reality check about how good he has it. When he works two days a week and starts complaining about not getting enough sleep, my jealousy often drives me to point out that most of us have to get up early five days a week not just two.

Jealousy makes us normal too. It is normal to be jealous of your brother or sister, and it feels good to feel normal. But the intertwining of jealousy and guilt is pretty difficult to separate and, more often than not, I feel stupid and bad for being jealous of someone who struggles so much.

But that isn't to say jealous feelings don't creep into lots of my interactions with my brother. Sometimes it takes all my strength not to fall into one of Phill's more annoying traits and make a comparison to myself every time he complains or brags about his life. I've found it does help, however, to talk about the feelings his comments elicit in me.

With autism, one thing is easy to forget, though it is surprising because it is so pervasive: people with autism don't recognize the effect their comments have on others. Phill is generally perplexed when what he says annoys me and makes me jealous. If I talk with him about it, saying, "When you say that, it makes me feel..." instead of snapping at him, he hears it and tries to explain what he means. It is helpful for me to talk about how I feel and it is useful for him to hear the impact his words have on others.

Fear

I have a lot of fears in relation to my brother and our relationship. Fear is one of the feelings I deal with the most now, as an adult. I'm probably more of a worry-wart than most people. But I'm willing to bet that some of these fears, while they might not be as ever-present as they are for me, keep us all awake at night with the sheer weight of them.

My fears related to Phill often manifest physically — my stomach aches when I think about his future. I vacillate between my fear he will never be able to live on his own, independent from his loving-but-often-overprotective family; and my equally palpable fear that he will live on his own and be exposed to a world that does not know how to deal with him and to people with no scruples, eager to take advantage of someone who is unquestioningly trusting.

I'm afraid he won't find something he wants to do with his life — something he can be passionate about. I am terrified he won't find someone to love — which is what he wants most in this world.

Even in the mundane details of day-to-day life, I am fearful for Phill. When he takes the bus home from Seattle, I ask him to call me so I know he is on the bus, and I often call to ensure he makes it all the way home. He's been riding the bus by himself since high school. He knows how to read a bus schedule and to understand bus routes, and he knows what to do to get home if a bus doesn't come, or is running late, or he ends up somewhere he didn't intend. But it doesn't matter — I still worry.

Fears like that are important to keep in check. I don't want to give Phill the impression he can't handle things or do things on his own, or that I don't believe in him. On the other hand, vigilance isn't a bad thing, and trusting my gut about safety rarely steers me wrong.

For myself, I worry about whether I can handle taking care of Phill when our parents are no longer able. Will I do it well? Will I give him what he needs and wants, keep him safe and allow him his independence at the same time? And, can I keep my sanity and my own life intact — take care of myself and Phill in equal measure?

My fears are some of the things I have to struggle to keep in check the most. When they take hold, I can become too controlling. One red flag that indicates when I'm being too fearful and over-involved in Phill's life is when he responds, "Ok, Mom." The sarcasm is palpable, and he is quick to tell me to back off. I think it is a good indicator for both of us. For me, I'm reminded he is an adult and can do for himself. For him, there is a rekindled desire to stand on his own two feet and make decisions on his own. My well intentioned but slightly suffocating concern for him causes him to assert his independence.

When I am really being honest with myself, it is clear my most pressing fear stemming from Phill's diagnosis of autism is not related to Phill at all. As I mentioned before, when I consider starting a family, I am fearful I will have a child of my own with autism.

Twin and familial studies have shown that genetic factors play a significant role in autism. Not to say that everyone with a person in their family with autism will have a child with the disorder, but the risk of it occurring is higher than in the general population. I don't know if I can care for a brother with autism and a child with autism at the same time.

That being said, my options are not to have children or to roll the dice and hope my child doesn't have autism. Currently there aren't any genetic tests to determine whether I am predisposed to have a child with autism. So there really isn't any way of knowing or making informed decisions.

It would be scary to allow that one fear to rule my life and dictate whether I have children. The only way to handle this concern in a healthy manner is to weigh the pros and cons. I have to be informed about the risk: even though the likelihood a person with a sibling with autism will have a child with autism is greater than the general public, the risk is still relatively low. I can also consider options like adoption. I can weigh how important it is to have a child of my own versus having an adopted child or not having children.

I will also need to talk to my doctor about my fears and listen to the advice, given my family history. Ultimately, it will be an emotional decision, and there isn't anything wrong with that. What matters is that I am making a decision with my eyes wide open.

In the grand scheme of things, the not-so-good feelings don't outweigh the good feelings I have when it comes to my brother. The majority of the time I feel pretty lucky to have him in my life. The important thing, in my mind, is to accept that sometimes I do have the not-so-good feelings. I'm not perfect and I can't expect myself to be patient, gracious, and forgiving every second of every day. If I held myself to that standard, I would constantly be disappointed, and ultimately I would probably fail to take good care of my brother. The job isn't being perfect. The job is being there for Phill.

THE JOB

At the age of six, I knew I would always have a role in caring for my brother. The exact moment I became aware of the fact I would someday be the main person responsible for him is unclear to me. I think it was not a light bulb going on as much as the sun rising slowly in the early morning hours; it was a slow awareness that started as a single ray of light and grew to a much brighter, clearer understanding after a long while.

This wasn't a surprise, by any means. I have always taken responsibility for Phill in a variety of ways, careening along the line between sister and parent, probably veering onto the parent side more often than either my brother or my parents would like. However, the dawning of realization of the prospect of doing this job all by myself added a sense of gravity that I had not fathomed when I was younger.

I think, and I hope, that over the years I have learned to temper my "rightness" and need to direct Phill's life. I am by no means perfect, and definitely overstep my bounds and am overly protective of Phill. Even now, when he is thirty-one years-old, I try to be aware of my role and let him live his own life.

I'm always going to be involved, but it is my wish to relinquish some of my efforts to control Phill and his choices. I want to be more sister than parent. What I am trying to resolve now is whether it is possible to act like his sister and his friend and take on the role of caretaker as well. Phill says I still overstep that line more often than necessary. His exact words are, "Kristen, I'm thirty-one. I don't need you telling me what to do. You don't have to be my mom."

That begs the question, however, of what is the job of being Phill's caregiver? In some cases, caregiver means full-time, daily living assistant - a person who helps with cooking, cleaning, sometimes even bathing and basic hygiene tasks. In other situations, like ours, caregiver denotes the person who is more symbolically responsible. The caregiver in our family is the person who looks after Phill's financials and monitors his safety. Currently, and perhaps in the future, it means living in the same place with him. For the most part, the role is not literally taking care of him; he takes great umbrage at the thought that someone else is in charge of his life. Instead, it is about offering him assistance in navigating the portions of life that are challenging for him and giving him as much autonomy as possible on everything else.

According to the Autism Society of America (ASA), a survey conducted in 1996 found that in 20% of homes in America - 1 out of 5 - someone is a caregiver either full or part time. That was almost 20 years ago and those numbers can only have gone up since then. There are literally millions of people who have assumed or expect to assume responsibility for a sibling with a significant mental or developmental disability. But there isn't an accurate count of these people because nobody keeps track of this population. Obviously, this is a big portion of society doing a job that isn't going away. And yet, that same ASA study found that only 20% of families with children with special needs — again, only 1 in 5 families — have done any planning to support that child for the rest of his or her life.

There are a plethora of responsibilities included in this new job that I will someday be shouldering. I have identified three major responsibilities as Phill's primary support person that I may assume: managing his finances so he has money to live on throughout his life, ensuring that he has suitable housing, and making certain that his days are active, through work or otherwise.

Money, Money, Money

The first, and by far the most important, is being accountable for his income, whether it comes from the government, a trust fund, his job, or some other source. This is the most pressing for a number of reasons. Phill has not been good with money. When he has money he wants to spend it (as we all do). Usually he does, most often on "stuff" (clothes, movies, video games), without a very clear awareness about what he might need in the future (rent, food, activities he enjoys).

Money makes everything else possible. I'll need to ensure that he has money for short-term wants and needs that make his life enjoyable and to keep him housed and fed. He will need money to enjoy pleasant experiences in the future and have the resources he needs throughout his lifetime.

Managing his finances is critical because it can impact his eligibility for government services, and more importantly, his ability to retain his health insurance to receive his medications.

In the last year or so, in conjunction with his job at my office, Phill has gotten much better about saving money. He thinks more carefully than he used to about what he spends his money on. I've been very impressed with his restraint and his efforts to think about his choices before he makes a decision. He's proud of his own growth in this area too. He loves sharing his thought process about how he has chosen not to purchase something now because he is saving up for a different item. However, his own long-term needs and savings requirements are still not concepts he grasps, and thus I will need to stay focused on these aspects of his finances.

I am definitely not a math wiz. It makes me nervous to balance my own paltry checkbook, and I pay someone else to do my taxes. Now, I will be juggling my own finances as well as the many sources of support, with the strings attached to them, of Phill's money as well. How does a person who is basically afraid of math take on this job? Research, research, research. I need to understand the rules, and plan to keep a folder or a binder with this information on hand so I can refer to it if I have questions.

There are some important pieces of information anyone can gather, places to focus research, and questions to ask that will lead to the road of understanding the job of caretaker.

First, know the rules for any programs from which your brother or sister is receiving services, including asset allowances, formulas for cash grants, and eligibility criteria. In addition, try to stay up to date on any changes to the laws related to those services as it might change your siblings benefit level or eligibility. Many disability advocacy organizations have legislative updates that you can receive via email or see online to track those kinds of changes. Similarly, be clear on how your siblings' special needs trust or a trust of any kind works.

Key questions to ask about trusts or any money set aside for your sibling include: How do you withdraw money? Can you deposit money? Is there a penalty for taking out more than a certain amount? Who has the authority to withdraw money? What happens if you are not able to fulfill your duties? Who is the second in command? Does the trust earn money on its own? Is it earning interest? Can you invest that money, and would that be wise? How can that money be spent? This might be stated in the trust and also may be further restricted or clarified in IRS and other government regulations. How much does your sibling earn through employment? What other benefits does he or she receive? Are there any other places where your sibling receives money?

Trusts and anything requiring a legally binding document are notoriously difficult to understand and navigate. In my research, every expert recommends hiring or meeting with a special needs lawyer who can accurately walk you through the maze of options, regulations, and other governmental rules that may apply to ensure that any wills and trusts set up for your sibling have been created appropriately.

In the resources section at the back of this book are websites and books that provide more detailed information about wills and trusts and other life planning topics. These will be of great use when you need them.

An important basic piece of information, at least for people residing in the United States, is that people with special needs cannot have a normal trust and still receive government benefits. The key to a special needs trust is that it does not belong to the person with a disability; it belongs to and is administered by someone else. In Phill's case, that someone would be me.

In our situation, Phill would be the beneficiary of the trust, which would be clearly delineated in the text of the trust itself. However, it is important to remember that most governments have strict requirements about trusts of any kind, including special needs trusts, and it is imperative that the trust be worded correctly, which is why consultation with a special needs lawyer is so important.

Every time the laws change, the rules around eligibility and qualifications may change as well. Only a lawyer who specializes in this area of the law will be able to fully advise on what will work best for your particular situation, for the state or country you live in.

The focus on wills and trusts is all well and good if parents are able to leave money to you or your sibling. But what if your family is not that fortunate? Whether your siblings have a trust or not, you must ensure they are receiving the government benefits for which they qualify. While my brother will have money set aside to help with his living expenses, he would not have health insurance were it not for the Medicaid coverage he receives from the U.S. government. He cannot be named in my parents' or my insurance because he is too old, and he doesn't receive benefits through his part-time employment.

The first thing to do is make sure your sibling is receiving any and all eligible benefits. No one relishes the idea of relying on government aid, but it exists to help when you have exhausted all other options. You and your sibling should not hesitate to use it if you need it.

Other assistance may depend on plain old ingenuity. If your brother or sister lives in a rented home or apartment and needs to spend less on rent, could a reduction be arranged with an offer to help out with property maintenance, like painting or yard work? If your sibling needs new clothes for a job interview, is there a nonprofit that helps disabled or low-income people acquire new or gently used suitable work clothing?

Do you attend a church that would be willing to collect donations to help you add onto your house so your sibling could live with you? Do you have friends who could donate labor, expertise, and materials to significantly decrease your cost of making room for your brother or sister?

A good resource when you are trying to figure out how to juggle all of the financial responsibilities and stretch every last dollar may be your local or national autism or disability advocacy organization. They may offer tips or, better yet, be able to link you directly to resources you can use.

Home Sweet Home

The second most important issue, in my mind, is that someday I will be in charge of Phill's housing. Housing is an important factor for people with autism because there are so few resources available, at least in the U.S., for those who cannot live independently. At this point in our family, we simply don't know at this point whether Phill can live independently or not so I need to consider all of the possible eventualities for where Phill will live.

According to Mary McHugh in her book Special Siblings, in 2003 at least 60,000 individuals were on waiting lists for government-funded housing programs in the United States. Her interview with the Executive Director of the ARC of New Jersey (the state affiliate of a national advocacy organization for individuals with disabilities) revealed that the waiting lists average three to four years for emergency cases and seven to nine years for non-emergencies. Almost ten years waiting for your sibling to have a place to live is a long, long time! There need to be alternative plans in place.

Housing may be a consistently big responsibility or may be relatively innocuous. Right now, my brother lives with our mom and step-dad, which is not his preference. He wants to live on his own. If he eventually gets into an apartment, condo, or house of his own, and flourishes, this job won't be that big for me. I will need to check in on him, help with maintenance issues, remind him to wash his dishes before ants arrive, and so on. Not a difficult role, and definitely the way that I hope it goes.

However, this maintenance may not be so idyllic, which hatches the "what-ifs". What if he attracts people with bad intentions or who are bad influences? Will I need to check in everyday to make sure he hasn't unwittingly allowed someone to deal drugs out of his apartment or steal his TV? What if his slovenly habits, overall noisiness, or some other factor get him evicted? Where will he transition easily into a new place? Will he be able to find a new place? What if he really isn't suited to live alone? Could he have a roommate? How will we find someone who is a good fit? What will make him happy? Could he live in some sort of supervised housing? Where do those opportunities exist and how much do they cost?   And of course, the biggest what-if: what if he needs to live with me permanently? Phill doesn't need to live in a fully staffed residential facility, and there aren't very many intermediate steps for him. The choices that appear to be available currently for him are living on his own or living with a family member. If housing isn't seamless, then some of these what-ifs may very well come to fruition and that will make the housing responsibility more regular and more stressful.

How do you prepare for the "what-ifs"? And what do you do if they start coming true? Whether or not your sister or brother lives with you now, if you think that someday they might, do yourself a favor and think hard about what makes the most sense for you and your family – your whole family. One of the houses I looked at many years ago seemed very nice, but all of the bedrooms were on the same floor. My brother is loud – and messy. If I owned that house and Phill moved in – even if it was for a few days or weeks – there would be no escape. That was not a situation that made sense for us at all. We would be at each others throats within hours.

Think carefully about what makes you crazy about your sibling and how a house you are considering would help or hinder your acceptance of that quirk or behavior. Consider too what your sibling might need. I seriously contemplated homes that had a separate entrance near the room that would be Phill's, because I know how important his independence is to him and I want to foster that if he ends up living with me.

One idea that I considered regarding Phill's living situation is unconventional, but it is something others might want to think about. As I mentioned, I have ample space for Phillip right now, but it isn't exactly a space of his own. My dad has been adamant that Phill have his own "piece of the pie" as in ownership of something that grows in value and is an asset for him in the future. In addition, we have struggled as a family to work out a transition plan for Phill to move out of our parents' house and live on his own.

With this goal in mind, I've thought about building a garage with a self-contained apartment above it as a transitional living space for Phill. It would provide me with an extra room if Phill moved out, but also maintain a place where Phill could always come back if that was necessary. The interesting part of this idea is that my dad would pay for the building on Phill's behalf, giving Phill a percentage of equity in my house. It wouldn't be money he could easily access, obviously, because I would have to sell the house for him to recognize his investment. Yet, it would essentially offer space that he "owns", could come back to whenever he wanted or needed to, and that would be building equity for him. Phill has expressed some interest in this idea, though it is still not his first choice. He says that he wants to live on his own, without family "breathing down his neck". But he is also a big fan of having a backup plan, and this one appeals to him.

I have to be honest though. Despite the fact that I helped come up with it, I'm not totally sold on this idea. There are a number of things to consider, the first of which, as my father pointed out, would be that I am essentially taking on responsibility for my brother starting right now. I don't know if I want to do that yet.

I don't know that I want to take the reins from my parents before I need to. Another issue is whether that is making it a little too easy on Phill. It is important to all of us that he makes an effort in his own life. If we provide him with this option, will he ever move out on his own, or make an effort to be successful if he does try living somewhere else? I would hate to unnecessarily limit his independence. On the other hand, I think it is an intriguing idea that potentially solves a number of problems: providing Phill with some assets, transition out of our parents' house, interim housing at other times in his life, and permanent living space, if necessary.

A Hard Day's Work

The third major component that I think about seriously is how Phill will fill his days. Right now, Phill gets paid to work at my office two days a week and spends half a day a week volunteering at the zoo. He loves his time at the zoo, but half a day once a week is all they can offer him because they try to accommodate so many people with an interest in volunteering there. This situation is working out well, for the time being, but I think everyone is clear that it is not a permanent solution.

I like having Phill with me, and I appreciate his help on different projects, but I also recognize that he might be better off working somewhere away from me and that my boss probably won't be able to keep paying him forever. I will not always work at this job; presumably when I leave, he will need to leave as well. I can't guarantee that my next employer will be as gracious as my current one.

Phill has ideas about what he would like to do. He has worked with a state agency designed to help people with disabilities find jobs with the hope of finding a more permanent full-time position. They have helped him with the job search, but have not succeeded at finding him meaningful work. Through the Goodwill job search program, Phill did find a job on an assembly line for a while. It was a good fit and Phill enjoyed it. However, the line closed down and moved out of the country. I don't know if Phill is the kind of person who will find a job or career and stick with it, or if he will move through a variety of jobs with varying degrees of success. So far he has bounced between volunteer and paid positions. Maybe that will be his pattern.

Phill's job prospects and the other things that fill his days are a major area of attention for two reasons – because I know it is important to Phill to be earning money and doing something that contributes, and because he needs to have a significant portion of his week filled with structured activities. Otherwise he'll end up sitting in the basement watching TV all day and not interacting with anyone which besides being unhealthy, tends to exacerbate his autistic behaviors. When I say "doing something that matters" I don't mean that he needs to be helping people or curing cancer necessarily, but rather that he needs to do something that means something to him. I don't know that this is what Phill wants to do for the rest of his life, but that something makes him feel good about himself makes me ecstatic.

He has started talking lately about needing a new job. While in the first moments that hurt my feelings a bit, I quickly realized what a huge step that was for him to realize on his own. He says he'd like to make more money, which he acknowledges means he needs to work more than twice a week. He also said, "You probably aren't going to be here forever and I need to do something on my own." That is an incredible level of self-awareness and motivation for Phill to recognize, which I think is fabulous. Still, I don't know if he will ever find something that he looks forward to doing, that he has passion for, or if that is even a priority for him. I also don't have any idea how to help him find that type of job.

How to help your sibling find a job is a difficult thing to give advice about. There should be an organization that has relationships with a large number of varied types of employers willing to hire someone who has autism or a developmental disability, that has job coaches who can go out with clients to get them settled in new jobs, offer them tips and pointers for how to succeed in the new environment, and troubleshoot both for the client and for the employer if problems or misunderstandings arise. Currently, at least in Washington State, this does not exist, except in the case of narrow bands of disabilities.

In lieu of that, the first step is to talk to friends and family. You might have friends whose company has a job or volunteer opening or who know of a good position for your sibling. Next, investigate any services offered in the area where you live. Maybe there are organizations in your state that can do the type of coaching and job assistance I mentioned.

Another option is to help your sibling by simply pounding the pavement with them, figuratively and literally. Read books with them or on your own about getting people with autism into the workplace. Some titles are in the resources chapter. Help your sibling create a resume and cover letter and understand what these are for. Sign them up — with or without you, whatever works best for you and your sibling - for classes that will help land a job. These types of classes are typically offered at community colleges, advocacy organizations, social service agencies, or through welfare or employment services offices. They highlight topics such as how to interview, what to say on an application, what to wear at an interview, and how to follow up with a prospective employer. Go online with your brother or sister and look at online job sites. Help them find jobs that might suit their interests and qualifications and post their resume, if appropriate.

Finally, consider options that don't involve your sibling getting paid. Be creative. Maybe he or she can work a few days a week; what will occupy time the rest of the week? Consider volunteer opportunities that relate to your sibling's interests or talents. Phill loves animals, which is why the zoo is such a great opportunity for him. He could also potentially work at the Humane Society, a veterinarian's office, at a groomer, or pet daycare center.

The trouble with some of those options is that Phill prefers not to interact much with strangers. This may not be an issue once you talk to the organization, but it is an important factor to take into consideration. For instance, at the zoo, Phill doesn't give tours, though that is one volunteer opportunity. Instead, he observes the animals and writes down what they do every five minutes for three hours. This meets his need not to talk to people, and also is well suited to his obsessive nature. He rarely, if ever, misses a five-minute check, right on the dot.

His responsibilities at my office are also well suited to his strengths. I had a file cabinet full of printed documents that we wanted to have accessible to the public. Phill catalogued each and every item in that file cabinet with all of the pertinent information (title, author, date of publication, keywords, topic, etc.) in an electronic spreadsheet. His ability to do a task repeatedly and not get bored made this a fantastic opportunity for us to have a digital database, and for him to feel he'd accomplished something. This wasn't a job that we had originally thought to give to a volunteer because it seemed so monotonous; it was one of those things we had on a wish list that was on a back-burner. Phill was the perfect fit for the job. Once he was finally done after many months, compiling the list of more than 2,600 articles, we had other projects that had been saved for "someday" which we could give to Phill.

So be creative. Think about what your sibling is good at and what not so good at. Play to strengths, and have patience. While these opportunities in which Phill is currently involved may not be permanent, they are something, and for now, that is enough.

Everything Else

These aren't the only issues I am going to struggle with as Phill's caregiver. There are other everyday issues to consider, and there are some big scary things I will have to think about and navigate, without having the control over them the way I might over finances or housing.

The mundane issues will work themselves out with only a

modicum of frustration. Things like groceries and meals and laundry and chores and showers (particularly if you have only one bathroom) are things that need to be negotiated, depending on the living situation. When Phill stays with me now I buy all the groceries, but if we go out to eat, he pays for himself about half the time. When we are at work, he pays for his own lunch, as that was part of the agreement with my boss for his getting paid. If we do an activity, like going to the movies or going to the driving range, he usually pays for his portion – probably about 80 or 90 percent of the time. However, when he isn't working a lot of those things change. I tend to pay for activities and meals out and Phill brings over his own food when he is eligible for and utilizing food stamps. It all depends on what makes the most sense so that he is offering a contribution to the whole.

He has a specified time when he needs to shower, excluding the time we are getting up to go to work, and he is good about sticking to it. If he stays over on non-work days, we negotiate by the timeline or activity of the day. If he ever moves in permanently, however, one of my first priorities is building another bathroom; sharing a bathroom is an issue that I feel could create problems on a regular basis, so I want to avoid the frustration entirely.

As a permanent resident, he will also be responsible for his own groceries. If I become more in charge of his money, that may require him to give me a list of items ahead of time when I am going shopping and taking that money out of his account, or assisting him with doing his own shopping. I could either drop him off at the store or take him with me so he can buy his own needed items. He tends to eat whatever is in sight, so this is another area we want to be clear on from the beginning to avoid unnecessary arguments and aggravation.

If your sibling will live with you full time, you will need to consider issues like this. You will also need to think about how your brother or sister is going to "split" the bills with you. For instance, if your sibling receives government assistance or has another income source, it is reasonable to pay something for rent, food, activities and so on. In fact, in all likelihood it will be a necessity for your sibling to spend down their government stipend because if they have more cash on hand than is allowed under the asset guidelines they can lose their eligibility for those services. Some of these items are easy to work out, as I have outlined above. Some are a little more complicated. You will have to decide how much is fair to charge for rent, what portion your sibling should pay for utilities (water, heat, electricity, etc.), and whether or not to charge something for gas if your sibling uses your car or can't drive and needs to be driven most places.

Then you need to agree on some ground rules. Who showers when? When is it ok to do laundry? Who is responsible for laundry? What happens when the dishwasher is full? Are there chores that your sibling is responsible for? If so, which ones, and how often are they to be done? Is there a curfew or time that everyone needs to be home at night? What are the rules about checking in if you aren't at home? Do you have such arrangements, or is your sibling responsible for his or her own time completely?

If your sibling doesn't live at home with you, these questions may simply be starting points for you to consider as a part of your role in your brother or sister's life. You may use them to prompt suggestions if your sibling is living independently. I don't often ask Phill about laundry or curfews because he lives with our parents, but I have asked him about what he thinks his responsibility is as a person living at our parents' house, especially at times when he has not been willing to do any of the chores our mom has asked him to do.

There are other issues that will come up. However, they may not going to be quite as easy to navigate. For instance, I wonder how I am going to help my brother deal with the death of one of our parents when I am going to be distraught myself. In particular, I wonder how to help him when I know how much he hates talking about or acknowledging intense emotions. In conjunction with that, if he has not already transitioned to another place to live, there may be a period of significant chaos in his life, and helping him through that will be a big job. As with most individuals with autism, Phill does not do well when his schedule and life are disrupted or significantly changed. I anticipate this being a very difficult time in both our lives and I think it is important to consider how to best facilitate and manage that time.

The last significant issue I want to touch on is the question of what happens when I am gone. This book addresses the issues of what to do when your parents are gone, but in many cases older siblings are caring for younger siblings and thus, there is a good chance the caretaker will die before their brother or sister with autism. Even without considering age, there is always a chance that something could happen to you, leaving your sibling without your assistance.

Sometimes there are other siblings who could or would be responsible for your brother or sister. In our family, we don't have any other blood siblings. We have a step-sister and step-brother who are very dear to us, but we have never discussed what their role in Phill's life might be were I not around. I don't know that they would feel the same responsibility or willingness to assume care for him that I do, or that Phill would be comfortable with one of them in that role.

In our family, we've determined there will always be two people in control of Phill's life, legally speaking, and we have determined a succession plan that begins with both of my parents, and moves to one of my parents and me when one of them dies. We have decided that it makes sense to have three living guardians legally identified at all times, so when one of my parents passes on, the surviving two guardians will name a third. This may not be a strategy that works for everyone, but it is one way to handle this issue.

You may have a spouse or other close family member who could be considered as a potential guardian for your brother or sister after you are gone. You may also consider your own children, depending on their ages. Again, this is a question that doesn't have an easy answer. Just as your parents need to have a solid plan in place for your sibling once they are gone, you too need to consider the other options for your brother or sister if you are no longer able to care for them.

I cannot anticipate everything that a person will need to think about or may encounter when taking on the role of caretaker for a sibling with autism. In fact, I can guarantee that no matter how much you've planned, how carefully you have thought about all sides of the situation, or how diligently you have prepared for this new role, you will encounter some surprises. The best advice I can give to deal with those inevitable unexpected issues is to be flexible and not be too hard on yourself. Give yourself permission to work through things slowly, to try out solutions, and to do something different if the first thing you try doesn't work. Allow yourself to make mistakes and give yourself time to work out the best situation for you and your sibling.

BEING MYSELF AND BEING HIS CARETAKER

The hardest part of taking on the job of caretaker is my fear that being Phill's caregiver is all that I will ever be. In some ways I know that is a silly thing to think; I will always be my own person and have my own thoughts, emotions, and interests. But in other ways, there is a risk I will become consumed with ensuring that his life is everything it can be and that I will neglect myself and my needs in an effort to meet his.

I've seen parents who become so consumed by their child's needs and desires that they seem to only exist through their connection to their child's accomplishments. I am desperate for this not to occur to me, and I'm not the only one.

Originally I thought I was going to name this book "My Brother's Keeper" but Phill didn't like the term "keeper". When we would talk about this book, he continually tried to think of other options for the title. One day he said, "I don't think you should call the book 'My Brother's Keeper'. I think you should call it 'My Brother's Helper' because I do things for myself". Ultimately, he was right, so I changed the title and he was right about the actual job too. I am not going to be his keeper because I do not intend to dictate what he does with his life; he has free will, which he is bound and determined to exercise, as well he should. He sees me as a resource, a place to go if he gets stuck or needs help, but not a person to give him permission to live his life.

The other day when it was cold and blustery, I asked him where his coat was. He very calmly said, "Kristen, I am thirty-one years old. I don't need you to tell me when I need a coat and when I don't." I think that is a sign of a healthy relationship.

Balancing Act

Trying to walk that line between helping and being controlling is hard. I am always fearful about whether I am overstepping my boundaries or not being vigilant enough. I also vacillate between my concern that I'm not being focused on my life enough in favor of ensuring his needs are met and that his needs are being neglected because I'm too focused on myself. Being afraid is justified and probably a good thing. Feeling a tension between Phill's needs and my own means I am reaching some kind of balance; a lack of either tension or fear would mean I had gone too far in one direction or the other. It is easy to wrap myself up in the life of someone else, both because I am invested in how well he succeeds, and also because it is a lot easier than focusing on the issues in my own life.

The question is how to prevent it. The very first step is to remember what Phill said: I am a helper, not a keeper. He does things for himself and I am simply an assistant. I cannot, and should not, for the most part, stop him from making decisions for himself, whether I think they are good or bad. I can help to guide him; I can offer advice; and perhaps I can dissuade him from making decisions that might cause him harm or do significant damage to him. Otherwise, I need to respect that he is an adult with thoughts and feelings and plans of his own.

Balance needs to be the key. For me, there has to be a balance of my needs and those of my sibling. Balance between helper and keeper. I absolutely know I will not be any good to Phill if I am not taking care of myself.

Fear of Failure

Here is my biggest, scariest secret about being responsible for my brother: I am terrified that I am going to totally and completely screw it up. Deep down in the places I don't like to talk about, I have visions that I mismanage Phill's trust, he gets kicked off of SSI, he doesn't have a place to live and moves in with me, I can't manage a relationship or a marriage because of the stress and the strain, and my brother and I fight constantly because I am too overbearing and he is too irresponsible, and we have no where to turn for help.

What if I am totally incapable of handling it all? I'm an overachiever. I cannot fathom failure. Yet, when I envision this job, failure is the first thought that pops into my head. Granted, this is not a useful mindset and I try to snap myself out of it when I catch myself wallowing in these thoughts. It isn't healthy for me, and it doesn't do any good. It is far better to focus on how to make sure those things don't happen, to prepare ahead of time for the responsibilities and have some plans for where to get support when I need it.

One way that I keep my fear in check is by talking about it. It is important —actually imperative — to talk to other people. It helps keep the fear from taking me down with it, and it helps ensure I have balance. Talking out loud to friends, a significant other, a therapist, a support group, or a life coach helps bring perspective, possibilities and support. I can talk to these people about the struggles and how hard it is, the cool thing my brother said the other day, or what I am feeling. Whatever I do, I say it out loud. That is important. That makes the fear feel not so big. If, when it comes out, the fear is still big, I have people who can help me deal with it and figure out a solution, or commiserate, or just acknowledge that it is hard.

I know I can't cut my friends out of my life by assuming they won't understand my commitment or by believing I don't have time for friends. I have to make time and make them understand. We all need an outlet, or else all that stuff - all those feelings, fears, frustrations - will build up and explode out of us in a wholly unhealthy and inappropriate way.

Talk to Your Parents!

Regardless of whom you choose to talk to about your fears and your feelings, the people you absolutely must talk to when taking on, or even considering this new role, are your parents. It is certainly not an easy topic to bring up, nor is it comfortable to sit down and discuss your parents' finances, your sibling's future, or your own life goals and intentions, but it is a necessity.

Talk to them about how you feel being responsible for your

sibling. Talk to them about your fears. Discuss your parents' intentions for your sibling after they are gone or can no longer care for him. Find out what benefits your sibling receives, when it comes and in what form, and the rules around it. Find out if your parents have put away money you need to be aware of. Discuss what they are planning for your sibling's life and how you factor into it. That is probably the single biggest thing that will help ease some of the fear and stress that come with this new role.

It is a good idea to bring the brother or sister whose life will be impacted by these decisions into the conversation as well. In some cases, depending on the characteristics of autism that your sibling possesses, it may not be possible to include your brother or sister in all of the discussions. But at whatever level is appropriate, incorporating your sibling in the process of deciding what is going to happen in his or her life is key. This inclusion is imperative because individuals with autism do not deal well with change, and preparation may help to remove some of the anxiety of that eventual change. Also, it honors your sibling as a human being and a participant in his or her own life.

Phill has very definite visions of what he wants from his life. Not taking his thoughts and feelings into consideration doesn't acknowledge his independence or self-awareness. At the same time, he doesn't like talking about topics that are uncomfortable, preferring to go away and consider one issue at a time and come back to tell us what he thinks, as opposed to being part of brainstorming and problem solving conversations. So in our family, we have meetings and Phill makes the decision about how included he is. When he reaches a topic he wants to think more about or when he gets overwhelmed, he steps away from the meeting and we continue. He comes back when he's ready.

When I suggest you talk to your parents, I mean all of them. These days many families are made up of more than just the nucleus of birth mother, father, daughter and son. In my family there are step-parents on both sides. It is important to hear what everyone envisions for your sibling and how they see themselves in his or her life and in your life. What if your birth parent dies before their spouse and their estate is left to their husband or wife? If your brother lives with your mother and step-father (as mine does), will your step-father expect to continue to care for your brother if your mother is no longer around? Does he plan to financially contribute to his future with the money from your mother's estate? These are important things to take into consideration when discussing the future.

I am including excerpts of a letter I wrote to my parents requesting just this kind of conversation. It wasn't easy to write, and it took me almost three months to send it, but I'm glad I did. Feel free to use it for inspiration if writing a letter to your parents to start the conversation seems safer or easier than talking face to face.

Mom and Dad,

I wanted to write you a letter because I feel like whenever I bring up the subject of Phill's future, one or both of you either try to reassure me there is nothing to worry about or you change the subject.

I am scared. The more I think about how I am going to balance my life and Phill's life, the more terrified I become. I know that you are trying to protect me, and I appreciate that. But I shouldn't have to remind you that I have never been one to languish happily in the dark – I can always come up with the worst case scenario and I will always take it upon myself to worry about the details of whatever comes my way. That is my burden to overcome, but your trying to shield me or protect me is not going to make me forget that someday you will not be around to care for Phill, and I will.

My major concerns are about Phill's inheritance, Phill's living situations, and Phill's livelihood. I know that we do not typically talk about money in this family, but I think that I need to understand how much money you believe Phill will need for the future, how that amount was reached, and how Phill is going to have access to those resources without losing his health insurance and other benefits.

Dad, I know that you told me Phill has a trust, and that it isn't a special needs trust. I did some research on special needs trusts and what I discovered is that basically, if something happened to you tomorrow, Phill w o u l d   b e kicked off SSI and he would have to spend down his entire inheritance/trust before he could be eligible for SSI again, at which point he would probably need to be on a waiting list for a few months before he could start receiving benefits again. Health insurance is very important for him, particularly with the medications he needs to take. We need to be sure that he has a trust that will not make him ineligible for services. That means not just talking to your lawyer, but to a lawyer who specializes in special needs trusts, because apparently they are very complicated and the laws change frequently, so we need to be sure that it is set up correctly.

In that same vein, Mom, I need to know what your intentions are. And, I need to know what happens if both of you are gone and one or both your spouses is surviving. I don't want to think about these things, and I don't want to be morbid, but much as I love Marcia and Brian, I know that they are not Phill's parents and may not want to have control of his life after you are gone. How does inheritance work in that case?

And what about housing? I know he wants to move out, and we want him to move out, but so far, nothing has happened with that. I am totally supportive of him moving out of the house and living on his own, but I think it is fair for us to have a conversation about what happens if that doesn't work out.

The one time I wanted to talk about this with you, Dad, when we were discussing having a place for Phill in our new house, you wouldn't even consider the idea that he might live with me. I think that it is naïve and unrealistic to not consider this option at all. There are not a lot of housing options out there for people like Phill. I wish there were, and I think it would be best if he could live on his own, but I also think we need to be honest about all of the options and plan accordingly.

And, I know, Dad, that you would like him to own his own house or condo. Again, I fully support this option – I want Phill to be independent too – but do we even know if he is allowed to own a home and still receive SSI? I don't think we are even going to know all of the questions until we sit down and talk about it.

I need you both to realize and believe that I am an adult and, much as you may dislike it, I am a part of this decision making process. I need you both to wrap your minds around the fact that while I am your child, I am also your successor of sorts, and I have a right and a need to be a part of planning for the future.

I love you, and honestly, more importantly, I love Phill, and I want to do right by him. The only way I think that can happen is if we carefully plan for the future, and then hope that the need for those plans is many years down the road.

I love you. Kristen

My parents responded quickly when they received my letter, and with much aplomb. While they did take issue with the implication that they pat me on the head and tell me to run along when the subject of Phill's future comes up, they acknowledged that they have put off the conversation.

In particular, my mother had this to say in response to the letter: "There's no way to express the chagrin I felt at being called to task for minimizing Kristen's needs as successor guardian for Phill. I know it was our desire to protect her and our own feelings of having plenty of time that aggravated our seeming unresponsiveness to her need for things to be planned well into the future. It was indeed startling to see for myself how the impact of my inaction caused distress. I'm grateful Kristen didn't give up and that she could so clearly articulate her needs."

Turning Talk Into Action

My mom and dad are incredible people and, true to form, once presented with my fears and my desire for some resolution, they immediately set a time for us to all sit down and talk. We had an agenda of what we wanted to discuss, though I don't believe that all meetings have to be that formal. However you have the conversation, it should be in a format with which you and your parents are comfortable. Just ensure that the discussion results in you getting the information you want and need.

We sat down to dinner – Mom, Dad and I. Interestingly, both of my step-parents thought the conversation should be just between us, so they chose not to join us, at least the first time. We talked about our fears, my fears in particular, and we discussed the major topics that we want to be sure to talk about over time – those things that can't be solved in one sitting.

Our focus was on Phill's trust because it seemed to be the most pressing issue, since we did not have the right vehicle in place to protect him at the time. My parents ventured outside their comfort zones, to their credit, to talk frankly about money and what they envision for Phill's future. They gave me room to vent my fears, and we set up a plan for talking about these issues every three to four months so we can avoid any of us feeling overwhelmed or frustrated. The plan is to meet by phone twice a year and face-to-face twice a year, focusing each meeting on one topic (housing, jobs, etc.) so we can spend enough time on each item to find some workable options or solutions.

While the first meeting with my parents certainly didn't solve everything or assuage all of my concerns, it did go a long way to making me feel like I'm not in this alone.

The first topic we covered after our initial meeting was a support system for me. That wasn't my priority, but my parents felt strongly that my feeling safe should be one of our first orders of business. The idea we came up with could be utilized by other families as well.

We determined that I needed a variety of supports, and the types of people I needed to include depended in part on what situations might arise. I knew I would need emotional support, but at times I may also need assistance from lawyers or accountants or other professionals. I might also need help from people outside my traditional circle of friends or family.

We created a list of all the people we could think of who might be willing to be a part of my support system. That included my close friends, the special needs lawyer my dad hired, Phill's SSI contact person, friends of my parents, and relatives. My parents decided to call each person on the list personally to ask them if they would be willing to participate in my network. We decided to leave it up to participants as to how involved they wanted to be.

We also developed a menu of ways people could participate. Options included things like: being available in an emergency, providing emotional support for me, helping find resources for particular crises (like housing), providing some respite for me, etc. Giving people choices ensured that they knew what was being asked of them and that they felt they could handle the responsibility they agreed to. It also suited people's personalities and particular situations better than just asking for a vague commitment. For instance, my mom has a friend I feel very comfortable with, but who is out of town a lot. By giving her options, she could stay a part of the support system without feeling as if she had to change her own lifestyle.

My parents also felt it was important to keep the network participants engaged, so we decided that we would send an email newsletter out to everyone once a year or so, around Phill's birthday to give an update on what is going on with Phill, what his successes and struggles have been over the past year, where he is living, and the like. I think it is an easy way to stay in touch and keep people up to date on our lives.

I found it both comforting and empowering to feel that my parents recognized my role in Phill's care and to know they heard my fears. The big issues don't need to be resolved all at once – what matters is that the conversation happens and that the lines of communication are open.

Obviously, just talking about the future isn't going to solve every problem or ensure that you are able to keep a perfect balance. I mentioned at the outset that one of the outcomes of Phill's diagnosis for me has been that I don't even consider taking jobs outside of Washington state so I stay close to him and my family. While that is true, I think it is an important issue to revisit because it speaks to the issue of not losing myself in my brother's life or diagnosis. You don't have to tailor your life to your brother or sister.

My jobs have always revolved around policy and legislative advocacy. Therefore, many of the best job opportunities come up in Washington DC, the nation's capitol. I have looked at some of those job openings, and even considered applying for a few. So far, none have enticed me enough to send my resume. That isn't to say that one won't someday.

Because I know that my brother doesn't deal well with change, I am reluctant to make a change in my own life that could result in major upheaval for him; still, change isn't out of the realm of possibility. While it may be difficult, I know that he would survive. And, if I would be happier, then ultimately I think that Phill would be happier as well. I think it is vital to be clear with myself and my family that I can't and won't subvert my dreams and aspirations purely to accommodate Phill. That is really the key.

I want to live in the city or state where Phillip lives because I like it here, because I have a good job, because it is a good place to raise a family, and, as a bonus I am close to my brother. But if I had decided to live close out of a feeling of guilt or oppressive responsibility, I think it would have been something to reconsider. Certainly my parents and my brother are grateful for my help, but it isn't the only thing that matters in this world.

Being True to Yourself

I have chosen to take on responsibility for myself. My parents were very clear that this is my decision, and I came to the conclusion that this is what I wanted on my own. If you resent the idea of feeling you are on call to take care of your sibling, or if you simply don't want to be involved in that way, that is a fair thing to think and to say. Don't try to be your "brother's keeper" because you think you have to be. That's not good for either of you.

There are places you can pay to take care of him, or other ways to shoulder the responsibility without being the person who is physically face-to-face with him on a day-to-day basis. You have to make the situation work for yourself and your own unique needs.

If your family lives in Minneapolis and you have a great job in New York, consider your options. Maybe your sibling can move to the city you're in, either to live nearby or to live with you. Maybe you can hire a home healthcare nurse to check in on your sibling on a regular basis or find a living situation that provides appropriate care based on your brother or sister's needs. Don't assume that you have to give up everything so that they can have every need met. It isn't worth it, and it probably isn't what your sibling or your parents would want for you.

Another issue that relates to your life is what you do for pleasure. What are your hobbies? What do you do to relax? What do you like to do to pamper yourself? These are things I believe should be fiercely guarded and never surrendered. When the pressures of life start building up, we often try to think of things we can discard to ease the burden a little bit. However, usually the first things to go are the things we want to do not the things we feel we need to do.

If my week is filling up and I have too much on my plate, the first things to go are exercise, reading, painting, and any unrestricted down time. While sometimes it is necessary to cut back on the things we enjoy or do for fun in order to meet all of our commitments. I believe we need to be very careful that temporary reductions in those activities don't become permanent.

I love my brother, and I love spending time with him, but sometimes I have to tell him that I can't do all the things he would like me to, or that he may have to do some things on his own. The same is true with my parents. I try to give them some time to themselves away from my brother, but I can't always accommodate their vacation schedules or get Phill to or from a given activity. While it may not feel good at the time to say no to your sibling or your parents, it is perfectly acceptable. You should have your own life, and respect your own interests. Make sure to schedule time to do the things that you love, and don't give up that time without thinking long and hard about it. If you aren't re-energizing yourself with the activities, places, and people that bring you joy, what do you have left to give your sibling?

Sometimes, reaching the balance between being yourself and being his caretaker is not a job you can do alone. It definitely isn't a job I can do by myself. I am often too close to the situation to realize when I have crossed the line, particularly in the direction of losing myself in favor of caring for Phill. While I may complain about my parents' being overly protective of me, their concern and care ensures that I don't take on this new, huge responsibility too soon. This has been a great gift.

It's challenging, certainly, but it's been useful that my parents haven't let my helping nature interfere with my ability to have my own life. They were always very clear with me that I should go away to college and take a job wherever I wanted. No one insinuated or expected me to move back to Washington after college. My parents helped instill in me at a very early age the balance and sense of self that is going to sustain me when I actually do take on responsibility for my brother.

My friends also provide a good barometer for whether my ability to balance my roles is skewed. It is clear that I am overly involved in my brother's life and losing sight of myself when I haven't seen my friends for a long time. I usually see my friend, Jeannie, at least once a week. If I haven't seen her in a while, I know I'm not paying attention to my own needs.

My friends are also great sounding boards for whether an idea makes sense. After I mentioned to Jeannie one thought about how I could take on more of my brother's housing needs, she said: "You are going to have your whole life to care for your brother, fifty or sixty years. Why would you take that on before you have to?" That isn't to say that her concern changed my mind about my idea, but it did give me pause, and remind me to keep the big picture in focus, not just the immediate solutions. Friends can often provide perspective that can't be seen by anyone living with a person with autism day-in and day-out.

A GUIDE FOR PARENTS

This chapter has two purposes. First, it is for siblings who are going to be taking on the caretaker responsibility. I hope it will help you start or continue the conversation with your parents about your impending role in your brother or sister's life. It may offer potential discussion topics, spark questions you seek to have answered or just give you an idea of what your parents might be going through during this transition.

The second use for this chapter is for you to give it to your parents to read. It may inspire them to plan a little more, or in a different way, or just to think about the future. Or, perhaps it will help them be more comfortable discussing your role as caretaker or their own feelings about giving up that responsibility.

Parents of special needs children are an amazing group of people, in my experience. They work hard to create a life that is fulfilling, accessible, and matched to the needs of their disabled child while at the same time they strive to meet the needs and desires of their typically developing children. To me this is a difficult balancing act, and I honor the creativity, compassion, tenacity and countless hours it takes.

Innocence vs. Information

In our family, our parents did not treat us equally, but they always treated us fairly. That is to say that, though we were not treated the same, our needs and wants were met in equal measure. My parents, like most parents of kids with special needs, not only spent an inordinate amount of their time meeting the needs of their children, they also spent time planning for how all of their children's desires would be met after they are gone.

To ensure that we are taken care of in the future, my parents have considered a variety of options and made decisions they felt made the most sense for our situation. My father set up trusts for us that we will have access to upon his death. The only thing I knew about the trusts before I started to write this book was that mine was structured so that I inherited a certain portion of the money at set ages – 25 and 30 for example.

My brother's trust, on the other hand, was set up with a trustee, namely me. For all of Phill's life, I would control the spending from the trust in consultation with him. I presumed that because the document had a trustee, it was set up specifically for someone with special needs, making it a "special needs trust" which I had heard about in passing. I appreciate my father's thoughtful planning. However, Phill's trust was not set up as a special needs trust, because my dad was unaware of the possible ramifications of a normal trust on Phill's government benefits and quality of life. I didn't know how much we would be inheriting. I wasn't sure if my dad had done any research on how much money to put in Phill's trust to cover a lifetime of needs. I didn't even know where the trusts were set up or who I would talk to if something happened to my dad.

While my brother lives with our mom, it's our dad who has always been Phill's financial support, and thus Mom has mostly focused on Phill's present while Dad planned for the future. My dad has extensive intentions for Phill, and laudable goals. The problem is that because it is a parent's job to care for all their children, sometimes he can't recognize eventualities involving Phill that need planning. Dad doesn't like the idea I would ever need to alter my life to accommodate Phill's. He doesn't want Phill to be a burden to me, and I don't want that either. I don't want to resent my brother or feel like I do not get the opportunity to live my own life because I am helping him live his. But I also do not believe that ensuring that we have discussed and planned for every eventuality is inviting trouble. I think it is the most probable way to guarantee that Phill does not feel like a burden to me one day.

My father didn't used to see it that way. The good news is that opinions can change. With time, and perseverance, Dad has come to understand that we have to discuss everything, even those options one or more of us may not want to have happen.

One thing I have learned from working through this process with my own mom and dad is how important and helpful it is for parents to talk to their children – all of their children – about the future. Parents who assume they are protecting their kids, especially the typically developing ones, by not talking about the future of the person with autism, may actually be doing them a disservice.

It may be true that the typical children will not need to care for their brother or sister. But it is far more likely they will play some ongoing role in the life of their sibling with autism and they need to know all of the facts in order to be effective. The thought process is often, "Oh, we'll talk about that later." But what if something were to happen now? What if "later" never comes? No one wants to think about that, and part of putting off the conversation probably goes back to the fear of burdening the typical child. But it is imperative for parents to think carefully about the weight of giving their child an understanding of their potential responsibility early (in young adulthood) when they have time to digest the information, consider their options, and plan, rather than having a huge responsibility dropped on them all at once with no preparation.

Planning for the Future

My parents' forethought and planning regarding to my brother's future, and their subsequent sharing of those plans with me, has been a significant contribution to my mental well-being and my ability to feel confident taking on this new role. In the last few years what we have learned is that even those things that we think are secure – like pensions and social security – may not be. Knowing that we may not be able to count on government support makes planning within our own families all the more necessary.

Parents with typically developing children usually plan their lives with the goal of not being a burden on their children in their old age. They focus on retirement, medical insurance, and life insurance, and making sure they have enough money to sustain themselves. Leaving a legacy or an inheritance for their children is something they'd like to do, but is not the priority. However, parents with a child with autism feel a stronger desire to leave resources for their children.

If parents start when their children are young, they can put away money for their child with autism as they would put away money in any other savings account or college fund. The Kidsource Forum website in the resources chapter includes a worksheet on how to determine the costs a child might accrue in their lifetime, in order to help establish the amount of money a parent might want to plan for.

There are also some options that may be available to help parents save and/or provide them with tax incentives for putting money away. Information on some of these options and resources to help them navigate through this process, regardless of their income, are in the final chapter of this book.

Many people will not have the luxury, foresight or ability to save for their children from the very beginning. If parents find themselves beginning this process at a later stage in their child's life, there are still things that can be done to help defray the ongoing expenses their child with autism will have in the future.

Life insurance policies, investments, and other opportunities that leverage some money to acquire more may be the best options when children are older and parents are nearing the end of their working life. If you use a formula to determine the support a child with autism might need for the rest of their life when you're starting to save, it may result in a figure that is daunting. The point is not that parents have thought of and can accommodate every need their child will have for an entire lifetime, but that they are doing whatever they can to help and are developing options ahead of time.

Most typical children do not expect their parents to have accumulated every dollar their sibling will ever need. It will be a comfort to them to know that their parents thought about the future and planned for it as best they could. A few steps that parents can take to plan for the future are: ensuring that their wills are set up appropriately, telling their children where all of their important papers are, and sharing their plans for life after they are gone.

Some parents do not believe they will need a trust of any kind, which may well be the case, but all parents should at the very least have a will. A will is important because it lays out the basics of what should happen with an estate upon the death of one or both parents. Parents might assume that their assets will simply pass down to their children equally, but this is not how estates without wills are typically resolved.

Without a will a person runs the risk of causing harm to their children because their assets could be frozen for an indeterminate amount of time while decisions are made about the estate. In addition, if assets are bequeathed to a child with autism who is receiving government services, and the dollar amount of the inheritance exceeds $2,000 (as of U.S. law in 2012), that child could lose eligibility for services.

Finally, if a child with autism will need someone else to act as guardian when the parents are gone, the parents' wills are the place to delineate who that successor should be.

Parents should consider consulting a financial planner or accountant regardless of their stage of planning so they can maximize their time and resources. In addition, it may make sense to meet with a lawyer who specializes in the particular issues that impact families dealing with a lifelong disability. They will help find out if there are other considerations they aren't aware of or changes to the laws since they began planning for the future of their child with autism.

If a family doesn't already have a lawyer or know one, deciding which lawyer to approach can be a difficult proposition. It is important to have someone who specializes in wills, trusts, and special needs issues. One way to find a reputable lawyer is for parents to go to any of the organizations they use and trust for other issues related to their child with autism. The local Arc, a local chapter of the Autism Society of America, Autism Society of Canada, or National Autism Society, or any support group or other advocacy group might have professional referral lists.

Asking other parents or siblings of a person with autism if they have someone they can recommend is also a good option. Alternatively, a parent could pose the question on a credible Internet listserv to receive advice. (A listserv provides an email list of management software to supply information.)

If none of those avenues pan out, there are some basic things to look for and ask about when considering a new lawyer. I asked a lawyer who is a member of the bar in Connecticut, New York, and Washington State to provide some advice for anyone considering hiring a lawyer sight unseen. Her tips are included in the resources chapter.

The Emotional Aspect

The final thing that my parents and I learned from dealing with these issues was that they needed to find a way to deal with the fact that I would be taking on the responsibility of caring for my brother, both functionally and emotionally. For my parents, this acceptance did not come overnight, and I expect that for any parent, it simply takes as long as it takes. It is important for parents to let their typical child take on some of the awareness and responsibilities piece-by-piece, as they are ready for it. Parents being able to let go and demonstrate a healthy understanding of this inevitability will make it easier for their children to do the same.

Just as I have advised that the typical child needs to acknowledge his or her feelings in regards to taking on this role, so too parents must explore whatever emotions handing over that job elicits for them. I can't accurately reflect what those emotions might be because I'm not a parent. However, I know at least two people who are intimately aware of the conflicting and sometimes overwhelming feelings triggered by the thought of this transition. I asked my parents to describe their own reactions, and this is what they had to say:

Dad's Response

To begin with, I suppose this is different for me than for Kristen's mom. I have really never been Phill's primary caregiver. I have been a source of financial support and, in some small way, emotional support for Phill. That said, this is a very complicated topic for me that gets caught up in a variety of other issues, all of which should be factored in to how it feels to me to hand off this responsibility.

The level of involvement I have had in Phill's life, the lack of a relationship between my wife Marcia and Phill, and the way I have felt the need to "manage" our family relationships as a result, are some of the things that factor in to my feelings about this issue. Compounding those pieces is the fact that I have had to move around the country to support the family, which has resulted in a lack of face-to-face contact with both Kristen and Phill as they were growing up. Added to that, of course, is the guilt resulting from the impact of our divorce on both Kristen and Phill.

I have always viewed my primary responsibility as ensuring that Phill has the necessary financial resources to meet his needs, without being a financial burden on those who otherwise support him. To date, I have done that with cash payments and support of his education. I have also made certain that I am well enough insured that, should I die unexpectedly, a reasonable level of resources would be there. Through the conversations we've had recently, it is clear that I now need to take additional steps, such as the formation of a special needs trust, to insure that he will be self supporting to the degree that my resources will allow. More than anything else, I believe this is my obligation to Kristen, not just Phill.

As it relates to my emotions regarding this hand-off process, I am delighted for Phill. Nothing could be better for him than to have his best friend be his partner in solving the problems, and issues that life will throw at him, but also, and as importantly, provide him with guidance and the willingness to share in life's challenges and joys.

As for Kristen, my reactions are decidedly mixed. I know that these are the kinds of challenges that she relishes, that this is work she's been doing her entire life, that this is more than an obligation for her – more than her "duty" — and I know it is an act of love, and that is why Phill is so fortunate. However, I am sad for the fact that I know this may be a limiting factor in her life. Phill's presence will draw some boundaries around the choices she will allow herself to make.

All I have really ever wanted for my children is for them all to have an unlimited array of life choices, and it saddens me to feel that Kristen's may be limited. On the other hand, you cannot know how much pride and admiration I feel for her. While I would not have expected less, her grasp of the issues facing her and Phill, and her willingness to take them on now, is remarkable.

There is a rather stunning feeling of helplessness when I think about these issues. I am used to solving problems, but this one is not mine to solve. I can only help facilitate a process that is inevitable. Nothing in my life has ever been quite like this. It has also caused me, once again, to consider my own mortality. Ironically, when I had cancer, I was so focused on healing and surviving, that once I figured out that everyone would be all right financially, the consideration of my mortality did not consume a lot of my energy.

This, on the other hand, requires that I consider a world in which I do not exist. It is about matters of legacy, and preparation, and protection for those that I love when I am not there to personally intervene. Not particularly frightening, but certainly sobering thoughts. It is also a completely unique perspective from which to view the turning of events. I cannot tell you the net of those thoughts, because the process is still under way, but I will say it is a challenging, enlightening, and a not totally unpleasant process.

Mom's Response

The only constant in parenting a child with autism is perpetual challenge. When Phill was young, I was convinced that his life would be better, maybe even normal, if only I knew enough. When he was school-aged it was about finding the right program, advocating for the best services, protecting his self esteem and striving for a typical childhood. Some years it was about mobilizing education personnel and teams of specialists. Some years it was private programs to protect against uninformed staff and inappropriate services. Some years it was simply managing Phill's behavior as best we could, collectively clenching our teeth, and desperately hoping for someone or something to shift for the better.

One of the things that helped me get through Phill's childhood was believing that my job ended when he reached adulthood. I thought it's much easier to be a quirky adult than to be an odd child. I hoped that constantly exposing Phill to ideas, hobbies, activities, and adventures would stimulate an interest, skill set, or passion which could override his disabilities and give him a niche in the world that could possibly lead him to a career, a partner, and independence. We're still waiting.

I gradually came to understand that Phill's adulthood would be as atypical as his childhood. And with that understanding finally came my awareness that no amount of my personal knowledge, research, advocacy, or buffering would override the impact of Phill's neurology. His wiring would determine life to a far greater extent than all of my training, plans, support, mobilization, and love.

Which brings me to the real point – what's it like to be

participating in multigenerational support planning? Amazing... and challenging... and touching.

It's amazing because it is 25 years or so before I'd be likely to be thinking about or passing along responsibility. It's amazing because it was our then 28-year-old daughter who was the impetus behind the collaboration. It's amazing because of the incredible talent, cooperation, creativity, and generosity exhibited by Phill's closest network.

It's challenging because we have so little of substance to work with. We know that people with autism are likely to have long smooth periods where things go well, and sudden, disruptive periods that can last for months or years. We have seen glimpses of Phill's most vulnerable areas which can help us organize, but we can only imagine the rest – and it's impossible to problem solve what we can't conceive. It's challenging to structure a future that best supports Phill without unduly burdening Kristen.

My most pervasive emotions generated by this book-writing/future-planning process have been awe and appreciation. I'm awed by Kristen's great love for her brother which translates into a willingness to share her life with him. I'm awed by her many talents, her organization and communication skills, her dedication to designing a future that best supports all concerned, and her passion for alleviating the pain of other siblings through the writing of this book.

Because of Kristen's curiosity and precise documentation, all of the members of our family have developed greater patience and understanding for Phill and for all of the challenges and gifts of the past 31 years. There were many aspects of growing up with Phill and interactions between the step-families that were not pretty or easy. Examining our history has allowed for deeper understanding of Phill and of one another and furthered our release of regrets. There's been a rather wonderful catharsis as we all worked together.

I so wish that it weren't necessary for Kristen to be her brother's caretaker – and I so appreciate her commitment to being his guardian in whatever role is necessary. I rest more easily knowing he has her in his corner. Yet, I desperately want to lighten the long-term impact. I want Kristen to have the freedom of her own life – and the right and support to decrease her level of responsibility if conditions change. I hope that she will be able to put her needs and her family's needs first if she ever has to make a choice. It is my fervent desire that the safety web we build for Phill includes supports for Kristen and resources to supplant her, should the situation become complex and beyond what can be anticipated, or even to assist Kristen stepping aside guiltlessly should she change her mind.

Finally, I'm deeply touched by the experience of working as a team with Kristen and her dad and our respective spouses to secure a future for this guy. That a team is in place to create possibilities is a blessing of the highest order and it's such a relief!

The Importance of Parents

My parents' experiences are by no means unique. Everyone will have conflicting emotions about sharing or handing off this big responsibility. But passing the torch does not mean that parents don't matter or aren't needed any longer. Nothing can take away the importance of parents in all our lives, and their role is even more vital when they have a child with autism. The best way parents can provide for their children – whether they are developing typically or not – is to plan for the future and include them in the decision making process so that they feel prepared and empowered.

FINAL THOUGHTS

Taking on the responsibility for a sibling with autism is a big, gigantic, often terrifying thought. It isn't to be taken likely. I'm nervous, and not a little scared about the prospect of this new role, but I know that I have built, and am continuing to build, a solid system of support around myself. Phill and I are well loved – we're very lucky – and I know those people who love us will hold us in their hands and do their best not to let us fall.

This job is a journey. I know I will stumble. Together Phill and I hope to strike a balance and find success. The only way that will be possible is if I continue to acknowledge and accept my feelings about myself, my brother, my role, and his autism.

This may not be a job that any of us chose, but it is one that we willingly accept. None of us will do it exactly the same way, deal with it in the same manner, or handle it perfectly. The "how" is not important. It's that we are doing it that counts. All we need to do, and all we can do is love our siblings, trust ourselves, let others help us, and do what we can. That's all anyone can possibly ask, and it's enough.

RESOURCES

General

Autism Society of America

4340 East-West Hwy, Suite 350, Bethesda, MD 20814
Phone: (800) 3AUTISM
Web: www.autism-society.org
Provides resources and links to websites of interest and has a free e-newsletter on autism issues. It covers a number of autism related issues and offers fact sheets and information on a variety of topics. They have specific sections focused on families including siblings.

The National Autistic Society

393 City Road, London EC1V 1NG, UK
Phone: +44 (0)20 7833 2299 Helpline: 0808 800 4104
Web: www.autism.org.uk
THE NAS is the leading autism organization in the United Kingdom. Its website contains significant information about autism and support for people with autism. There is a special section for parents, relatives and caregivers with a separate page for siblings and a section for adults with autism. The NAS also provides a helpline for autism related issues and does advocacy work to promote policies that benefit people with autism; the website contains pages of links to other websites about autistic spectrum disorders.

Autism Society Canada

Box 22017, 1670 Heron Road, Ottawa, Ontario K1V 0C2
Phone: (613) 789-8943
Web: www.autismsocietycanada.ca
ASC is committed to advocacy, public education, information and referral, and support for its regional societies. The website includes links to provincial autism societies and information related to Canadians with autism. It is available in English and French, and includes a special section with resources and information for families and caregivers. They also have a resources section called Autism Junction.

The Arc

1825 K Street NW, Suite 1200, Washington, DC 20006
Phone: (800) 433-5255
Web: www.thearc.org
The Arc describes itself as "the largest national community-based organization advocating for and serving individuals with intellectual and developmental disabilities and their families". It contains a variety of resources on all different kinds of disabilities, but has a section on autism and provides a variety of web links, including specific sites regarding employment, training, and transitioning to work. Most states have multiple Arc chapters which can all be accessed on the main Arc website. Services provided by chapters include: financial assistance, employment services, caregiver support, legal and health care assistance, to name a few.

Autism Source (program of ASA)

Web: www.autismsource.org
Autism Source is a search engine that can provide you with local U.S. resources for a variety of issues including: community support, legal/advocacy, medical, dental, schools, and government agencies. You can search by keyword and by state, city, or zip code for services in your area.

Family Village

Web: www.familyvillage.wisc.edu

The Family Village is a website that "integrates information, resources, and communication opportunities on the Internet for persons with cognitive and other disabilities, for their families, and for those that provide services and support". The site includes resources on diagnoses, communication tools, adaptive products and technology, adaptive recreational activities, education, spirituality, health issues, disability-related media and literature, estate planning, and more.

Geneva Centre for Autism

112 Merton Street, Toronto, Ontario, Canada, M4S 2Z8

Phone: (416) 322-7877

Web: www.autism.net

The mission of the Geneva Centre is to "empower individuals with an Autism Spectrum Disorder, and their families, to fully participate in their communities". The website includes a special section for parents, and the Centre offers a number of services and resources in Canada.

OASIS@MAAP (Asperger's Syndrome and autism)

MAAP Services, Inc. P.O. Box 524 Crown Point, IN 46307

Phone: (219) 662-1311

Web: www.aspergersyndrome.org

The Online Asperger Syndrome Information and Support (OASIS) center joined with More Advanced Individuals with Autism, Asperger's Syndrome and Pervasive Developmental Disorder (MAAP) to create a single resource for families, individuals and medical professionals who deal with the challenges of autism and Asperger's. They have newsletters, articles and local resources.

National Dissemination Center for Children with Disabilities (NICHCY)

1825 Connecticut Ave NW, Washington, DC 20009

Phone: (800) 695-0285

Web: www.nichcy.org or in Spanish: www.nicncy.org/espanol/
NICHCY serves as a central source of information on: disabilities in infants, toddlers, children, and youth; IDEA, which is the law authorizing special education in the U.S.; and research-based information on effective educational practices. There is a special section for families (parents, specifically) and there are a number of online publications and information on issues related to disability.

National Institute of Mental Health

Web: www.nimh.nih.gov (search for "autism")
A Parent's Guide to Autism Spectrum Disorder: www.nimh.nih.gov/health/publications/a-parents-guide-to-autism.pdf
The NIMH website provides a lot of credible information on disabilities in general and autism specifically. Resources include articles and research related to the cause and treatment of the disability, information about medications, and congressional reports on the disease. THE NIMH also has a booklet available, specifically dealing with Autism Spectrum Disorders (see link above).

World Institute on Disability

Web: www.wid.org
The mission of the World Institute on Disability (WID) "in communities and nations worldwide is to eliminate barriers to full social integration and increase employment, economic security and health care for persons with disabilities". They have a variety of resources available including some about Individual Development Accounts which are noted below in the Wills and Trusts section.

Sibling Specific

Sibling Support Project

Web: www.siblingsupport.org
The Sibling Support Project is a program of the Kindering

Center and is "a national effort dedicated to the life-long concerns of brothers and sisters of people who have special health, developmental or mental health concerns". They provide sibling support groups throughout the world (called "Sibshops"). Sibshops exist in all 50 states in the US and in the District of Columbia. They are also offered in nine other countries around the world: United Kingdom, Ireland, Canada, New Zealand, Belgium, Guatemala, Iceland, Japan and the Philippines. They also host an online support group for siblings of individuals with disabilities called SibNet.

Barnardo's

Tanners Lane, Barkingside, Ilford, Essex, IG6 1QG
Phone: 0800 008 7005
Web: www.barnardos.org.uk
Barnardo's is dedicated to serving children in need throughout the UK. One of its focuses is helping children who are caring for sick or disabled family members. It provides sibling support groups across the United Kingdom and provides other services like counseling, assistance finding respite care, and opportunities to participate in recreational and social activities outside the homes.

Books for Siblings

What About Me? Growing Up with a Developmentally Disabled Sibling. Bryna Siegel and Stuart Silverstein, 1994.

The Ride Together: A Brother and Sister's Memoir of Autism in the Family. Paul Karasik and Judy Karasik. 2003.

Right Address...Wrong Planet: Children with Asperger Syndrome Becoming Adults. Gena P. Barnhill, 2002.

Sibling Stories: Reflections on Life with a Brother or Sister on the Autism Spectrum. Lynne Stern Feiges, Esq. and Mary Jane Weiss, Ph.D./BCBA, 2004.

Special Siblings: Growing Up with Someone with a Disability.

Mary McHugh, 2003.

<u>Living with a Brother or Sister with Special Needs: A Book for Sibs</u>. Donald Meyer and Patricia Vadasy, 1996.

<u>Thicker than Water: Essays by adult siblings of people with disabilities</u>. Edited by Don Meyer, 2009.

<u>How to be a Sister: A Love Story with a Twist of Autism</u>. Eileen Garvin, 2010.

Wills, Trusts, Jobs, Social Support and Books for Parents

Wills and Trusts: KidSource Forum

Web: <u>www.kidsource.com/kidsource/content4/estate.dis.all.3.3.html</u>

(This section was written by Richard Fee, of the National Institute on Life Planning for Persons with Disabilities.)

This website is an excellent resource for understanding estates, trusts, and wills. In particular, it is useful in explaining different types of trusts available in the U.S., how they function and what might work best for you. It also includes a worksheet for determining your child's monthly expenses, which will help with determining how much money your child will need to live in the future.

Wills and Trusts: The NAS Booklet

Web: <u>www.autism.org.uk/~/media/NAS/Documents/Get-involved/Leave%20a%20legacy/Guide%20to%20wills%20and%20trusts.ashx</u>

The NAS provides a booklet free of charge that provides information on the law in the United Kingdom. It is called "A Really Simple Guide to Wills and Trusts for People Living with Autism" and can be ordered or downloaded through its website. The booklet differentiates types of trusts that can be set up in the UK, and how they may impact the state services received by the individual with autism, as well as the pros and cons of having or not having a trust at all. This website also contains useful information on what Disability Living Allowance is and the eligibility criteria to claim the allowance.

Savings Option: 529 Plans

Web: http://money.howstuffworks.com/529.htm

In the U.S., there are tax-free options for saving for college. In particular there are "529 Plans" where there are no taxes on the account's earnings, you have total control over the money (not your child), and the money can be used at any age. The hitch is that this only applies to education. If you withdraw the dollars for non-education related use, you aren't penalized, but you will have to pay the taxes. I mention this account both because it could be a useful tool, but also because it is the impetus for a push in the US Congress to create similar tax free accounts for the other needs that children with disabilities in particular will have in their lives – many of whom will not be attending college, and thus cannot benefit from the 529 Plans. The site listed above will give you basic information on how these plans work, including state by state variations. You can also go to most financial planners and financial institutions for more information.

Saving Option: Individual Development Account

Web: Ledorf, World Institute on Disability, http://wid.org/publications/individual-development-accounts-a-golden-opportunity-for-persons-with-disabilities/ OR

Center on Budget and Policy Priorities 2002 Federal IDA Briefing Book www.cbpp.org/10-29-02wel.pdf

For low-income families and individuals with disabilities, there is the option of an Individual Development Account (IDA) savings program. This program helps people do things like buy a house or a car or start a business, and for every deposit made into the account, a matching deposit of one to three times the original deposit is also made. The only qualification is that the participant needs to be within 200 percent of the poverty level and have some source of earned income. There is a very useful guide created by the Center on Budget and Policy Priorities in

2002 called: 2002 Federal IDA Briefing Book, and it outlines how IDAs might impact public benefits. Specifically related to SSI, an IDA is not counted as part of a person's assets so long as it is funded under the federal law, Assets for Independence Act (AFIA). AFIA IDAs are safe for people with SSI to participate in and can be used to save for a home or other approved IDA uses.

Job Search: Goodwill Industries International, Inc.

Web: www.goodwill.org/goodwill-for-you/jobs-and-careers/
Goodwill Industries provides customized job search services for individuals and they specialize in helping people with disabilities find jobs. Their website provides some initial resources and tells you how to get in touch with the Goodwill in your area who can help you with your job search.

Books for Finding Jobs

How to Find Work That Works for People with Asperger Syndrome: The Ultimate Guide for Getting People With Asperger Syndrome into the Workplace (and Keeping Them There!). Gail Hawkins. 2004.

Developing Talents: Careers for Individuals with Asperger Syndrome and High-Functioning Autism. Temple Grandin, Kate Duffy, and Tony Atwood. 2004.

Social Support: Best Buddies International

100 Southeast Second Street, Suite 2200, Miami, FL 33131
Phone: (800) 89-BUDDY
Web: www.bestbuddies.org
Best Buddies assists with the creation of one-on-one relationships between disabled and non-disabled individuals. In addition, it provides supported employment in the US in Miami, Boston, and Los Angeles. The main office is in Miami FL, but there are offices in 21 other states and more than 47 other countries. It also provides "e-buddies" for online, email buddies.

Choosing a Lawyer

My friend, a lawyer admitted to the bar in Connecticut, New York, and Washington State provided some tips for choosing a lawyer. Her first piece of advice is to check with your city or county bar association when beginning your search for a lawyer. They may have a lawyer referral service through which you can get the names of lawyers in good standing that specialize in wills and trusts, and they may even be able to direct you to lawyers who have expertise in special needs trusts specifically.

Next, she says you should check out any lawyer you are considering working with through the state bar association. They will let you know if your lawyer has had any disciplinary actions filed against them. In addition, either the state, county, or city bar association may be able to refer you to services that may be free or low-cost if you are low-income. When you have narrowed down your search and are meeting with or speaking with a lawyer and deciding whether or not to work with them, here are some questions to start with:

- Do you specialize in trusts and estates?
- Do you specialize in special needs trusts and, if not, what experience have you had with special needs trusts?
- What memberships do you hold? (Meaning: what bars and associations are you admitted to.)
- Do you have a fee agreement in writing? (Most lawyers will have an agreement in writing that you can see which lays out how much they charge and what services they charge for.)
- Can you talk to me about how many hours you anticipate this process taking and give me an idea of how much that might cost?

Books for Parents

Asperger's Syndrome: A Guide for Parents and Professionals. Tony Attwood, 1997.

Siblings of Children with Autism: A Guide for Families. Sandra L. Harris, Ph.D. and Beth A. Glasberg, Ph.D., 2003.

ACKNOWLEDGEMENTS

I so appreciate my extraordinary family for believing in me. In particular, Mom and Dad: I am so grateful for your unwavering love, boundless encouragement, incredible strength, quiet patience, and willingness to open your private lives to the world for the greater good. You are more amazing than I deserve, and I can't express how much I love you both. Marcia, Sarah, Brian, and Ryan: it is an admirable thing to choose to accept new people into your family; thank you for allowing us into yours and for giving us so much love. Pierre and Amanda: I'm so glad my siblings were smart enough to marry you! And of course, Phill: you're right, this book couldn't exist without you. I am very thankful that you inspired it and that you are in my life. I am lucky to have you.

I am indebted to all of my friends for their offers to do anything and everything they can to help, and for their boundless enthusiasm. Chris, Joan, Nancy, Sophy and Maria: your astonishing support, advice, and expertise have been invaluable to me, and your friendship continues to sustain me. Jeannie: thank you for putting up with me through this process, for utilizing your amazing skills to make this book better, and for being such a consistent support in my life. Erin: It doesn't matter where I am or what I'm dealing with, you never judge, you always have time, and your love is unconditional; I can't tell you how important that is. Kealan: you never made it seem like my family was any stranger than anyone else's and you spent more time in the mayhem than most. I am so grateful to have had you for all of these years. Sarah: thank you for the emotional support you never fail to provide, for sharing this journey through life with me, for always accepting Phill as a part of the package, and for being such an amazing friend. Thank you. I love you all.

ABOUT THE AUTHOR

Kristen Rogers received her Bachelor's degree from Mount Holyoke College and her Masters in Social Work from the University of Washington. She lives in Fircrest, Washington with her dog Gus, close to her brother, mom and step-dad.